21
Jump-Start
Devotional

Books by Miles McPherson

21 Jump-Start Devotional

Bad to the Bone

The Power of Believing in Your Child

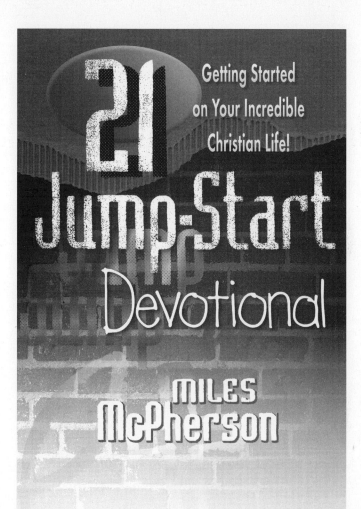

21

Getting Started
on Your Incredible
Christian Life!

Jump-Start

Devotional

MILES
McPherson

BETHANY HOUSE PUBLISHERS
MINNEAPOLIS, MINNESOTA 55438

Published by Bethany House Publishers
A Ministry of Bethany Fellowship International
11400 Hampshire Avenue South
Minneapolis, Minnesota 55438
www.bethanyhouse.com

Printed in the United States of America by
Bethany Press International, Minneapolis, Minnesota 55438

ISBN 0–7642–2146–9

A special thanks to

Wayne Rice

for all his help in preparing
this important tool for
new believers.

MILES McPHERSON was an NFL football player with the San Diego Chargers when he dedicated his life to the Lord. Before long, he felt the need to reach out to today's youth and preach the gospel to this lost generation. After earning a Master of Divinity from Azusa Pacific University, Miles began Miles Ahead Ministries, where he is now a featured speaker at some of the nation's largest youth events, including the Miles Ahead Youth Crusades. In addition to his work with Miles Ahead Ministries, Miles is associate pastor at Horizon Christian Fellowship in San Diego, California, where he teaches 2,700 people in a weekly Bible study. Miles and his wife make their home in San Diego with their three children.

For more information, contact

Miles Ahead Ministries
9888 Carroll Center Road #122
San Diego, CA 92126
619–271–0700

Or check us out at

www.milesahead.com

Contents

Congratulations!

You have just made the most important decision of your life. The impact of asking Jesus to be your personal Lord and Savior is beyond anything you could ask or imagine. To help you understand the impact, I want to tell you a story.

One Christmas morning, a little boy came running down the stairs looking for that special present he was hoping to get. His eyes scanned the gifts under the tree and suddenly his heart started racing! There it was! Just what he wanted! A GI Joe with the Electronic Kung Fu Grip!

But when he looked a little closer, his excitement turned into disappointment. He discovered that his new toy was broken. It had been damaged. His mother offered to fix it—to tape it together so that it would work for a little while . . . but the little boy said, "No!" He had his heart set on a GI Joe that wasn't broken.

All of us were once like that damaged toy. Because of sin, you were broken and unacceptable to God. And all your life Jesus has been waiting—not to patch you up or to tape you together—but to make you brand-new!

The Bible says in 2 Corinthians 5:17, *"What this means is that those who become Christians become new persons. They are not the same anymore, for the old life is gone. A new life has begun!"* This means that Jesus has forgiven you of all your sins and you are now ready to go to heaven. Because of what Jesus has done for you, you are a totally new person and you have a totally new relationship with God!

Back to my story.

The little boy did get his brand-new GI Joe with the Electronic Kung Fu Grip. He was so excited! But after getting it, he didn't want to just look at it or toss it aside. He wanted to enjoy it. He wanted to get the most fun out of it that he possibly could. In order to do that, he needed to learn how to use it, so he read the instructions and followed them carefully. After all, his mother paid big money for "The Big Grip."

In the same way, you will want to get the most out of your new life in Christ. Now that you are a brand-new person inside, you will need to learn how to live this new life. There are easy-to-understand instructions in God's Word, the Bible. It is important to read them and follow them carefully. After all, Jesus paid a huge price so that you could have your new life.

This book is designed to help you learn how to get started in your new life as a Christian. I hope and pray you will enjoy your relationship with God and the new life that comes with it!

See you in heaven,
Miles McPherson

Important Notice

If you are not sure whether you have asked Jesus Christ to be your Savior and Lord, but you would like to make sure, then say the following prayer. When you pray, make these words your own words. If you say them sincerely and believe them in your heart, you can be assured that God will hear and answer your prayer. These words are based on the true and reliable Word of God.

Dear God, I believe that I am a sinner, and because of my sin I deserve to go to hell. I believe that Jesus Christ is the only Son of God, and that He died and rose from the dead for my sins. I also believe that He loves me and gave His life for me.

Dear God, I ask, by faith, that you forgive me of all my sin and come into my heart. I receive Jesus Christ as my personal Lord and Savior. Please fill me with your Holy Spirit and take over my life. Change me into the kind of person you want me to be. Thank you, Lord, for saving me. Thank you for making me a true Christian!

Guess what? You're going to Disneyla . . . NO!

You're going to Heaven!

Say What?

How did that happen?

Here are ten important "Say Whats" for you to remember about your new relationship with Jesus Christ.

All you need to do is:

Say "What" ten times and you will learn the basics of your new relationship with Christ!

1. What you had

SIN. Just as every person you know breathes air, eats food, and needs to sleep . . . every person has sin in his or her life. Sin is not a white, brown, or black thing. It is not a male or female thing. It's a human thing.

Romans 3:23, "For all have sinned; all fall short of God's glorious standard."

1 John 1:10, "If we claim we have not sinned, we are calling God a liar and showing that his word has no place in our hearts."

2. What you had coming

ETERNAL DEATH AND SEPARATION FROM GOD IN HELL. Because of your sin, and because of God's perfection

(His holiness), it was impossible for you to have a relationship with God.

Romans 6:23, "For the wages of sin is death. . . ."

3. What you needed

PAYMENT FOR YOUR SIN. Sin is expensive. God requires that sin must be paid for. Not with money, of course, but with death. When you sinned, you were sentenced to receive the death penalty. But wait! What if someone else—who had no sin of his own to die for—died in your place? Only one person is capable of doing that. His name is Jesus Christ. He had no sin of His own, but He went to the cross to die for your sins. He paid the price so that you could live.

Romans 5:8, "But God showed his great love for us by sending Christ to die for us. . . ."

Romans 5:21, "So just as sin ruled over all people and brought them to death, now God's wonderful kindness rules instead, giving us right standing with God and resulting in eternal life through Jesus Christ our Lord."

4. What you needed to do

REPENT OF YOUR SINS. To repent means to change direction or to turn around. It means a willingness to turn away from sin and to begin living under the influence of God rather than under the influence of Satan.

Acts 3:19, "Now turn from your sins and turn to God, so you can be cleansed of your sins."

5. What you are

COMPLETELY FORGIVEN! In order for you to receive God's complete forgiveness, you must confess or agree that you are a sinner in need of forgiveness. Once God forgives you, your sins are gone. Forever! He will never bring up the subject of your sin again.

1 John 1:9, "But if we confess our sins to him, he is faithful and just to forgive us and to cleanse us from every wrong."

Psalm 103:12, "He has removed our rebellious acts as far away from us as the east is from the west."

6. What you will become

MORE LIKE JESUS. The word *Christian* means "Follower of Christ," and the whole purpose of giving your life to Jesus is to become more like Him and to honor Him by living according to His example and His teachings. If this sounds hard, remember that you don't have to do this on your own. God gives you the power of His Holy Spirit to encourage you and to work in you to live a successful Christian life.

Philippians 1:6, "And I am sure that God, who began the good work within you, will continue his work until it is finally finished on that day when Christ Jesus comes back again."

7. What you now have

A RELATIONSHIP WITH GOD. When you became a Christian, you entered into a relationship. Christianity is a relationship with God, not a religion. There are many religions, but there is only one way to have a relationship with God—and that is through Jesus Christ.

John 10:10, "My purpose is to give life in all its fullness."

John 15:14–15, "You are my friends if you obey me. I no longer call you servants, because a master doesn't confide in his servants. Now you are my friends, since I have told you everything the Father told me."

8. What your relationship with God is based on

THE UNCONDITIONAL LOVE OF GOD. God loves you because you are His beloved child. He loves you so much that He gave His only Son for you. He doesn't love you because you are talented, good-looking, nice, popular, or have important friends. He won't stop loving you if you become discouraged, angry, or disobedient. There is nothing you can do to make God love you any more or any less than He does right now.

John 3:16, "For God so loved the world that he gave his only Son, so that everyone who believes in him will not perish but have eternal life."

1 John 4:10, "This is real love. It is not that we loved God, but that he loved us and sent his Son as a sacrifice to take away our sins."

9. What you do in return

LOVE GOD. Above all the good things you could ever do as a Christian, loving God is at the top of the list. How do you love God? Here are just a few ways: by obeying Him, by being with His people (the Church), by spending time with Him in prayer and reading the Bible, by loving other people.

Matthew 22:37–38, "You must love the Lord your God with all your heart, all your soul, and all your mind. This is the first and greatest commandment."

1 John 5:3, "Loving God means keeping his commandments, and really, that isn't difficult."

10. What will keep you going

FAITH. Remember, God did not give you eternal life because you said the right words, went to the right meeting, or gave the right amount of money. He forgave you because you put your faith in Him. With this same faith you must walk with Him every day of your life. When things are going well, have faith. When things are going badly, have faith. Keep trusting Him and believing Him . . . by faith.

2 Corinthians 5:7, "That is why we live by believing and not by seeing."

Three Key Words to Remember

GRACE

The word *grace* describes God's unconditional love for you. Because of God's grace, you have been given forgiveness for your sins, friendship with God, and a future in heaven. You didn't deserve any of that, but God is a *gracious* God who loves you and wants to have a close relationship with you.

GRATITUDE

The word *gratitude* describes how we respond to God's grace. God paid a huge price for our salvation. We love Him, serve Him, and obey Him out of gratitude for what He has done. This we do by faith.

GROWTH

The word *growth* describes what happens to us when we respond to God's grace and demonstrate our gratitude to Him by loving, serving, and obeying Him. When you become a Christian, you're a lot like a newborn baby. You are dependent on others and vulnerable to danger. That's why it's important to read the Bible, to study and learn about your faith, and grow strong in Christ. God's Word is spiritual food. If you read it and apply it to your life, you will grow.

Six Simple Steps to Powerful Prayer

It is important that you understand what prayer is all about.

Prayer is communication with God. Prayer is when you speak to God and when God speaks to you. It is a two-way kind of communication. Funny, isn't it, that when we speak to God, we call that prayer. But when someone says God speaks to them, we call them crazy.

Throughout the Bible and all through history, God has spoken to people and given them direction. God wants to speak to you as well. God says in Jeremiah 33:3, *"Ask me and I will tell you some remarkable secrets about what is going to happen here."*

The main thing about prayer is to be honest and open before God with your feelings, thoughts, and desires. He wants you to come to Him and He wants to listen to you. Remember, when no one else in the world wants to listen to you, God does!

One way to pray is to just say AWCIPA. Listed below are six simple steps to powerful prayer. Spend a predetermined amount of time on each step before you move on to the next. This will allow you to focus your prayer time with the Lord. The six steps are:

1. **A**dmire God and thank Him for His love and His goodness.
2. **W**ait in silence for God to speak to you.
3. **C**onfess anything in your life which needs healing and forgiveness.
4. **I**ntercede for others you know.
5. **P**ray for yourself, your needs, and your wants.
6. **A**dmire God some more.

A Few More ?s You Might Have

What about church?

You might be wondering, *Now that I'm a Christian, do I have to go to church?*

Well, I have only one answer for you: YES! AND RIGHT AWAY!

Why?

First of all, because God commands it. Hebrews 10:25 says, *"And let us not neglect our meeting together, as some people do, but encourage and warn each other, especially now that the day of his coming back again is drawing near."*

But you may be thinking to yourself, *Wait a minute! There are too many hypocrites in the church!*

You're right. Not only are there hypocrites in the Church, but there are drug addicts, liars, backstabbers, and every other kind of sinner you can think of. These kinds of people are in church, and they're in your school, on your athletic team, on your job, and everywhere else.

But you still go to school, don't you? Why? To learn. And you go to work, don't you? Why? To make money. You still play sports and you still associate with people everywhere you go.

If sinners don't stop you from doing any of your other activities, then they shouldn't stop you from going to church.

Don't fall for the "hypocrite excuse" that Satan plants in your head.

The issue is not whether there are hypocrites in the Church but whether you are in the Church and if you will be one of those hypocrites. There are many people at church who, just like yourself, have a real desire to follow Jesus and be faithful to Him. There are many good people in every church who love God and have many years of faithful experience they can share with you. You can learn from them—but you need to seek them out and be where they are!

What is church, anyway?

First of all, you need to know that the Church is not a building, a place, or a religious organization. It is *people*. In the Bible, the word *church* actually means "called-out ones."

This means the Church is a chosen group of people—young, old, black, brown, white, rich, and poor—who have been *called out* by God from the population of the world to be His representatives on earth. They are *called-out ones* who love God, love each other, and serve God to the best of their abilities. Now that you are a Christian, you are one of the *called-out ones*. You are part of the Church!

A church *service* (in a church building at a particular time and place) is nothing more than where the *called-out ones* go to worship God together and to learn more about how to accomplish what they have been *called out* to do.

What will I get out of church?

Oops. Wrong question. If you go to church to "get something out of it," you won't get much at all. But if you go to church to grow closer to God by participating in the worship service, studying God's Word, and learning to serve Him—then you'll get more than you ever imagined was possible.

What is worship?

Worship is how we respond to God. When we attend a worship service, we are reminded of God's love, His goodness, and His holiness. Then we respond by worshiping Him.

One way to worship or respond to God is by singing songs of praise (Psalm 30:4). Another way is to hear and learn from God's Word (Psalm 119:9–11). We also worship God by participating in things like baptism (Acts 2:38) and communion (Luke 22:19–20). And it is loving other people (John 15:12) and serving them in the name of Jesus Christ (Matthew 25:31–40).

In reality, everything you do can be an act of worship—a response to God's love and holiness. Colossians 3:17 says, *"And whatever you do or say, let it be as a representative of the Lord Jesus, all the while giving thanks through him to God the Father."*

One more thing. We also worship God by sharing the Good News about Jesus with those who don't know Him as Savior and Lord (2 Corinthians 2:3–4).

But isn't Christianity a personal thing? Can't I just keep my faith a secret?

Consider this: If everyone else had kept their faith a secret, how would you have heard about Jesus? Just as someone shared Christ with you, you must be willing to share Christ with others.

Tell someone you know that you accepted Jesus. I know it's not easy at first, but allow the Holy Spirit to work through you to tell someone.

Let me explain by telling you about one of Jesus' disciples. His name was Peter. He walked with Jesus for three years. Jesus taught him about the Good News and performed miracles in front of him. But when Jesus went to the Cross, Peter denied that he even knew Jesus—not once, but three times in one night! It's hard to believe that someone like Peter would be such a coward.

But later on, after Jesus had risen from the dead, Peter was filled with courage. He shared Christ in the middle of Jerusalem and three thousand people immediately became Christians (Acts 2).

You may not be able to share your faith with three thousand, but you can share your faith with those you know. And remember, when you share Christ with others, you are not alone. Christ is with you and the Holy Spirit will give you courage.

Let me challenge you to tell others about your faith in Jesus. Practice explaining the Good News about Jesus with people. The better you can explain it, the better you will understand it and the more consistently you will live it.

Keep in mind also that the more people who know you have given your life to Christ, the more motivated you will be to live for Jesus when you are around them.

What if people ridicule me for being a Christian?

That's good! If you are ridiculed, put down, or cut off by others, you are in good company. All of Jesus' twelve disciples were persecuted (or killed, or both) for following their Lord. Jesus himself died on the cross as a result of persecution. Jesus said, *"And everyone will hate you because of your allegiance to me . . ."* (Matthew 10:22). As Christians, we consider it an honor to suffer a little for the One who suffered so much for us. The Bible says, *"Dear brothers and sisters, whenever trouble comes your way, let it be an opportunity for joy* (James 1:2). Expect persecution and ridicule and know that God will be with you in the middle of it all. He will help you to grow stronger as a result.

Now that I'm a Christian, will all my problems go away?

Sorry 'bout that. God doesn't take away all your problems when you become a Christian. In fact, sometimes you get even more! (See the previous question.) But in God's kingdom, bad circumstances are just opportunities to learn how to be dependent on God. What is the most common response people have when bad things happen to them? They usually cry out, "God, help me!" That's exactly what God wants you to do. He wants you to lean on Him and depend upon Him every day of your life, and He uses problems to teach you about yourself and your new life (see Hebrews 12:11). God wants you to:

- Wait for Him to give you direction, power, and courage (Psalm 46:10).
- Ask Him for wisdom and He will tell you "some remarkable secrets about what is going to happen" (Jeremiah 33:3).
- Trust Him and fight your battles in His strength and the power of His might (Ephesians 6:10–11).
- Know He will be there to encourage and comfort you (2 Corinthians 2:3–4).
- Know He is in control of everything. You can trust Him (Proverbs 3:5–6).

How do I become a disciple?

Excellent question!

The way you become a disciple (a Christ-follower) is to be *discipled* by someone else. Jesus commanded his original twelve disciples to go out and make *other* disciples (Matthew 28:19–20). Fortunately for us, they obeyed their Master and that's why we have disciples today. If you become a disciple, it is because the original twelve disciples "discipled" someone else, who in turn "discipled" others, and so on right down to today. This process is also called "mentoring."

I want to suggest that you find someone who will disciple

or mentor you in the Christian faith. Don't wait until something bad happens before you look for someone to give you advice and help. You should pray for a discipler—a mentor—someone who has been a Christian longer than you and whom you respect. Ask them to disciple you. Ask them to pass on to you some of their knowledge, wisdom, and advice from their life experience as a Christian (2 Timothy 2:2).

It would be ideal if you and your mentor could make a commitment to meet together for six months to a year. You might want to spend time together each week studying the Bible, praying, or just hanging out together. You can spend time together in ministry at your church, in the community, or on mission trips. This will not only help you grow as a Christian, but it will provide you with a strong support system when trials come.

Okay! I'm Ready to Grow!

But . . . How do I do that?
Introducing . . .

21 Jump-Start Program

Remember, Christianity is a relationship, not a religion. Jesus wants to get to know you as an individual, friend, and brother or sister. You need to get to know Him as well. What better way to get to know Him than to sit down quietly and let Him speak to you through His Word, the Bible. And what better time for this to happen than the first thing in the morning.

We will call this time your "morning devotions," a time of spiritual reflection. This is one of the most important habits to get into as a Christian. The process is so simple it can be outlined in three words:

Read•Reflect•Respond

Say it three times before you continue:

Read•Reflect•Respond
Read•Reflect•Respond
Read•Reflect•Respond

How Does This Work?

First, **READ** a section of the Bible.

Then, **REFLECT** on the message it has for you.

Last, **RESPOND** by writing down one way you will allow this message to impact your life, then follow through.

Let me explain this further.

Make sure you have a pen and paper with you every time you have your morning devotions. The more clearly you can write what God says to you, the more clearly you will understand. Also, when God speaks to you through His Word, it would be a shame to forget what He says, wouldn't it?

Now **READ** a passage (a few verses) from the Bible, several times if necessary, and be prepared to discover what it means for you. Remember, you are in no hurry, so relax your heart and your mind. Psalm 46:10 says, *"Be silent, and know that I am God. . . ."* Just Chill!

Now you are ready to **REFLECT** on the spiritual meaning of the verses. Ask God to show you what it is. Pray, *"God, please speak to me right now. Teach me what You want me to learn."* When God speaks to you, you should write it down. Again, the more clearly you can write what He teaches you, the more clearly you will understand and remember it.

Okay, it's time to **RESPOND.** Think of how you will incorporate God's Word into your daily life. Write it down. This is most important because this is what you will actually commit yourself to do. Take time to pray that God will give you the strength and wisdom to obey Him with this new information and direction for your life.

This book includes the Gospel of John from the the *New Liv-*

ing Translation. It is called "The Gospel According to John" because "Gospel" means "Good News." It is one of the four books of the Bible that tell the story of Jesus and His life while He was on earth.

Along with the Gospel of John, I have written twenty-one lessons to help you understand what God is saying to you through His Word. There is one lesson for each of the twenty-one chapters in John. If you will **READ** one chapter each day . . . and then **REFLECT** and **RESPOND** to the lessons provided, you will begin to grow strong as a Christian.

THE CHALLENGE:

It takes twenty-one days to form a habit. In the next twenty-one days, you will form the best habit in the world: *SPENDING QUALITY TIME WITH GOD*.

I challenge you to be faithful and read through the rest of this book over the next twenty-one days. Besides the satisfaction of finishing something that you start, you will gain a solid understanding of who Jesus Christ is and you will learn to read and understand God's Word. You will also learn how to listen to God and hear Him speak to you through His Word.

REMEMBER ... Read. Reflect. Respond.

• Chapter One •

Jesus, Like No Other

Read ...

Notice that Jesus was a most unique individual.

He was all God, yet He was all man. He came offering unconditional love and eternal life to all who believed in Him. How could anyone reject Him?

As you read this first chapter in the book of John, see if you can pick out the unique qualities that made Him *like no other*.

John•Chapter 1

In the beginning the Word already existed. He was with God, and he was God. ²He was in the beginning with God. ³He created everything there is. Nothing exists that he didn't make. ⁴Life itself was in him, and this life gives light to everyone. ⁵The light shines through the darkness, and the darkness can never extinguish it.

⁶God sent John the Baptist ⁷to tell everyone about the light so that everyone might believe because of his testimony. ⁸John himself was not the light; he was only a witness to the light. ⁹The one who is the true light, who gives light to everyone, was going to come into the world.

¹⁰But although the world was made through him, the world didn't recognize him when he came. ¹¹Even in his own land and among his own people, he was not accepted. ¹²But to all who believed him and accepted him, he gave the right to become chil-

dren of God. [13]They are reborn! This is not a physical birth resulting from human passion or plan—this rebirth comes from God.

[14]So the Word became human and lived here on earth among us. He was full of unfailing love and faithfulness.* And we have seen his glory, the glory of the only Son of the Father.

[15]John pointed him out to the people. He shouted to the crowds, "This is the one I was talking about when I said, 'Someone is coming who is far greater than I am, for he existed long before I did.'"

[16]We have all benefited from the rich blessings he brought to us—one gracious blessing after another.* [17]For the law was given through Moses; God's unfailing love and faithfulness came through Jesus Christ. [18]No one has ever seen God. But his only Son, who is himself God,* is near to the Father's heart; he has told us about him.

[19]This was the testimony of John when the Jewish leaders sent priests and Temple assistants* from Jerusalem to ask John whether he claimed to be the Messiah. [20]He flatly denied it. "I am not the Messiah," he said.

[21]"Well then, who are you?" they asked. "Are you Elijah?"

"No," he replied.

"Are you the Prophet?"*

"No."

[22]"Then who are you? Tell us, so we can give an answer to those who sent us. What do you have to say about yourself?"

[23]John replied in the words of Isaiah:

"I am a voice shouting in the wilderness,
'Prepare a straight pathway for the Lord's coming!'"*

[24]Then those who were sent by the Pharisees [25]asked him, "If you aren't the Messiah or Elijah or the Prophet, what right do you have to baptize?"

[26]John told them, "I baptize with* water, but right here in the crowd is someone you do not know, [27]who will soon begin his

---

1:14 Greek *grace and truth;* also in 1:17. **1:16** Greek *grace upon grace.* **1:18** Some manuscripts read *his one and only Son.* **1:19** Greek *and Levites.* **1:21** See Deut 18:15, 18; Mal 4:5–6. **1:23** Isa 40:3. **1:26** Or *in;* also in 1:31, 33.

ministry. I am not even worthy to be his slave.*" [28]This incident took place at Bethany, a village east of the Jordan River, where John was baptizing.

[29]The next day John saw Jesus coming toward him and said, "Look! There is the Lamb of God who takes away the sin of the world! [30]He is the one I was talking about when I said, 'Soon a man is coming who is far greater than I am, for he existed long before I did.' [31]I didn't know he was the one, but I have been baptizing with water in order to point him out to Israel."

[32]Then John said, "I saw the Holy Spirit descending like a dove from heaven and resting upon him. [33]I didn't know he was the one, but when God sent me to baptize with water, he told me, 'When you see the Holy Spirit descending and resting upon someone, he is the one you are looking for. He is the one who baptizes with the Holy Spirit.' [34]I saw this happen to Jesus, so I testify that he is the Son of God.*"

[35]The following day, John was again standing with two of his disciples. [36]As Jesus walked by, John looked at him and then declared, "Look! There is the Lamb of God!" [37]Then John's two disciples turned and followed Jesus.

[38]Jesus looked around and saw them following. "What do you want?" he asked them.

They replied, "Rabbi" (which means Teacher), "where are you staying?"

[39]"Come and see," he said. It was about four o'clock in the afternoon when they went with him to the place, and they stayed there the rest of the day.

[40]Andrew, Simon Peter's brother, was one of these men who had heard what John said and then followed Jesus. [41]The first thing Andrew did was to find his brother, Simon, and tell him, "We have found the Messiah" (which means the Christ).

[42]Then Andrew brought Simon to meet Jesus. Looking intently at Simon, Jesus said, "You are Simon, the son of John—but you will be called Cephas" (which means Peter*).

[43]The next day Jesus decided to go to Galilee. He found Philip

1:27 Greek *to untie his sandals.* 1:34 Some manuscripts read *the chosen One of God.* 1:42 The names *Cephas* and *Peter* both mean "rock."

and said to him, "Come, be my disciple." [44]Philip was from Bethsaida, Andrew and Peter's hometown.

[45]Philip went off to look for Nathanael and told him, "We have found the very person Moses and the prophets wrote about! His name is Jesus, the son of Joseph from Nazareth."

[46]"Nazareth!" exclaimed Nathanael. "Can anything good come from there?"

"Just come and see for yourself," Philip said.

[47]As they approached, Jesus said, "Here comes an honest man—a true son of Israel."

[48]"How do you know about me?" Nathanael asked.

And Jesus replied, "I could see you under the fig tree before Philip found you."

[49]Nathanael replied, "Teacher, you are the Son of God—the King of Israel!"

[50]Jesus asked him, "Do you believe all this just because I told you I had seen you under the fig tree? You will see greater things than this." [51]Then he said, "The truth is, you will all see heaven open and the angels of God going up and down upon the Son of Man."*

Reflect ...

The Bible makes it very clear there is no one else like Jesus. He was "with God" in the beginning, *like no other*. He "was God," *like no other*. He "made all things," *like no other*. He had "life to give," *like no other*. His life is the "light of all men," *like no other*.

But the sad thing is there are many people who reject this light. They are loved by God, made in His own image, and they don't even realize it. They don't listen to His voice; they don't obey His words. They go through life "doing their own thing." Basically, they have rejected God's love and have rebelled against Him.

1:51 See Gen 28:10–17, the account of Jacob's ladder.

Respond ...

Is there an area of your life that represents how you have rebelled against God? In the space below, write it down and pray that you will be able to give this area of your life completely to God.

_____

_____

_____

_____

_____

When you pray, ask God to make the next twenty days a wonderful experience for you as you grow closer to Him.

• Chapter Two •

Jesus, a Man Who Cared

Read ...

Jesus performed many miracles while He was on earth, and for many reasons. He did them to show His power over demons, disease, life, and death. His miracles were also a display of His love and compassion for people. In this story, no one is dying, no one is possessed by a demon, no one is in serious trouble. But Jesus still performs a miracle. Why? As you read, pray that God would reveal to you His reason for performing the miracle.

John•Chapter 2

The next day* Jesus' mother was a guest at a wedding celebration in the village of Cana in Galilee. ²Jesus and his disciples were also invited to the celebration. ³The wine supply ran out during the festivities, so Jesus' mother spoke to him about the problem. "They have no more wine," she told him.

⁴"How does that concern you and me?" Jesus asked. "My time has not yet come."

⁵But his mother told the servants, "Do whatever he tells you."

⁶Six stone waterpots were standing there; they were used for Jewish ceremonial purposes and held twenty to thirty gallons* each. ⁷Jesus told the servants, "Fill the jars with water." When

2:1 Greek *On the third day;* see 1:35, 43.   2:6 Greek *2 or 3 measures* [75 to 113 liters].

the jars had been filled to the brim, ⁸he said, "Dip some out and take it to the master of ceremonies." So they followed his instructions.

⁹When the master of ceremonies tasted the water that was now wine, not knowing where it had come from (though, of course, the servants knew), he called the bridegroom over. ¹⁰"Usually a host serves the best wine first," he said. "Then, when everyone is full and doesn't care, he brings out the less expensive wines. But you have kept the best until now!"

¹¹This miraculous sign at Cana in Galilee was Jesus' first display of his glory. And his disciples believed in him.

¹²After the wedding he went to Capernaum for a few days with his mother, his brothers, and his disciples.

¹³It was time for the annual Passover celebration, and Jesus went to Jerusalem. ¹⁴In the Temple area he saw merchants selling cattle, sheep, and doves for sacrifices; and he saw money changers behind their counters. ¹⁵Jesus made a whip from some ropes and chased them all out of the Temple. He drove out the sheep and oxen, scattered the money changers' coins over the floor, and turned over their tables. ¹⁶Then, going over to the people who sold doves, he told them, "Get these things out of here. Don't turn my Father's house into a marketplace!"

¹⁷Then his disciples remembered this prophecy from the Scriptures: "Passion for God's house burns within me."*

¹⁸"What right do you have to do these things?" the Jewish leaders demanded. "If you have this authority from God, show us a miraculous sign to prove it."

¹⁹"All right," Jesus replied. "Destroy this temple, and in three days I will raise it up."

²⁰"What!" they exclaimed. "It took forty-six years to build this Temple, and you can do it in three days?" ²¹But by "this temple," Jesus meant his body. ²²After he was raised from the dead, the disciples remembered that he had said this. And they believed both Jesus and the Scriptures.

²³Because of the miraculous signs he did in Jerusalem at the Passover celebration, many people were convinced that he was

2:17 Or *"Concern for God's house will be my undoing."* Ps 69:9.

indeed the Messiah. [24]But Jesus didn't trust them, because he knew what people were really like. [25]No one needed to tell him about human nature.

Reflect ...

Jesus' first miracle was turning water into wine. The Bible tells us that He displayed His glory with this miracle. But the story also shows that Jesus was sensitive to the needs of His mother and the people who were at the wedding. He simply wanted to make the wedding ceremony a joyous occasion. He wanted to bless the people who were being married.

Remember that Jesus wants to bless you, too. No matter what you are going through, nothing in your life goes unnoticed by Him. He cares about all of your affairs. You may not see water changed into wine, but you can have confidence that Jesus is involved in your life.

Respond ...

Can you name one situation in your life where you need His help right now? Describe it and write out what you need from Jesus. Is it wisdom, patience, love, the ability to forgive. . . ?

_____

_____

_____

_____

_____

When you pray, ask God to do a miracle in your life and to change you into the kind of person He wants you to become.

• Chapter Three •

A Baby Thang

Read ...

Many people think religion can solve the world's problems. Nicodemus, a well-educated rabbi (a Jewish religious leader), didn't understand why his religious training could not produce the kind of miracles that Jesus was doing. Nicodemus had more religious training than Jesus, but Jesus had more power than Nicodemus. Why?

Well, it wasn't "a training thang," "a money thang," or "a religion thang." What kind of "thang" was it? Read chapter three, focusing on the first nineteen verses, and you'll find out.

John•Chapter 3

After dark one evening, a Jewish religious leader named Nicodemus, a Pharisee, ²came to speak with Jesus. "Teacher," he said, "we all know that God has sent you to teach us. Your miraculous signs are proof enough that God is with you."

³Jesus replied, "I assure you, unless you are born again,* you can never see the Kingdom of God."

⁴"What do you mean?" exclaimed Nicodemus. "How can an old man go back into his mother's womb and be born again?"

⁵Jesus replied, "The truth is, no one can enter the Kingdom of

3:3 Or *born from above;* also in 3:7.

God without being born of water and the Spirit.* ⁶Humans can reproduce only human life, but the Holy Spirit gives new life from heaven. ⁷So don't be surprised at my statement that you* must be born again. ⁸Just as you can hear the wind but can't tell where it comes from or where it is going, so you can't explain how people are born of the Spirit.''

⁹"What do you mean?" Nicodemus asked.

¹⁰Jesus replied, "You are a respected Jewish teacher, and yet you don't understand these things? ¹¹I assure you, I am telling you what we know and have seen, and yet you won't believe us. ¹²But if you don't even believe me when I tell you about things that happen here on earth, how can you possibly believe if I tell you what is going on in heaven? ¹³For only I, the Son of Man,* have come to earth and will return to heaven again. ¹⁴And as Moses lifted up the bronze snake on a pole in the wilderness, so I, the Son of Man, must be lifted up on a pole,* ¹⁵so that everyone who believes in me will have eternal life.

¹⁶"For God so loved the world that he gave his only Son, so that everyone who believes in him will not perish but have eternal life. ¹⁷God did not send his Son into the world to condemn it, but to save it.

¹⁸"There is no judgment awaiting those who trust him. But those who do not trust him have already been judged for not believing in the only Son of God. ¹⁹Their judgment is based on this fact: The light from heaven came into the world, but they loved the darkness more than the light, for their actions were evil. ²⁰They hate the light because they want to sin in the darkness. They stay away from the light for fear their sins will be exposed and they will be punished. ²¹But those who do what is right come to the light gladly, so everyone can see that they are doing what God wants.''

²²Afterward Jesus and his disciples left Jerusalem, but they stayed in Judea for a while and baptized there.

²³At this time John the Baptist was baptizing at Aenon, near Salim, because there was plenty of water there and people kept

3:5 Or *spirit*. The Greek word for *Spirit* can also be translated *wind;* see 3:8. **3:7** The Greek word for *you* is plural; also in 3:12. **3:13** Some manuscripts add *who lives in heaven.* **3:14** Greek *must be lifted up.*

coming to him for baptism. ²⁴This was before John was put into prison. ²⁵At that time a certain Jew began an argument with John's disciples over ceremonial cleansing. ²⁶John's disciples came to him and said, "Teacher, the man you met on the other side of the Jordan River, the one you said was the Messiah, is also baptizing people. And everybody is going over there instead of coming here to us."

²⁷John replied, "God in heaven appoints each person's work. ²⁸You yourselves know how plainly I told you that I am not the Messiah. I am here to prepare the way for him—that is all. ²⁹The bride will go where the bridegroom is. A bridegroom's friend rejoices with him. I am the bridegroom's friend, and I am filled with joy at his success. ³⁰He must become greater and greater, and I must become less and less.

³¹"He has come from above and is greater than anyone else. I am of the earth, and my understanding is limited to the things of earth, but he has come from heaven.* ³²He tells what he has seen and heard, but how few believe what he tells them! ³³Those who believe him discover that God is true. ³⁴For he is sent by God. He speaks God's words, for God's Spirit is upon him without measure or limit. ³⁵The Father loves his Son, and he has given him authority over everything. ³⁶And all who believe in God's Son have eternal life. Those who don't obey the Son will never experience eternal life, but the wrath of God remains upon them."

Reflect ...

This is a powerful chapter from the Word of God. From it we learn that eternal life is not a "religion thang" ... it's a "baby thang!" Jesus told Nicodemus, "You must be born again." What He's saying is you must become reborn spiritually.

Your second birth happens when you believe that God loves you and that He sent Jesus Christ to die for you so that you can

---

3:31 Some manuscripts omit *but he has come from heaven.*

have a new life. Read verse 16 in this chapter again. This is a good verse to memorize.

As you go through the day today, keep in mind that you have been "born again," and you have become a new person with a new purpose, a new Father, and a new family.

Respond ...

In the space below, write out one way your life has changed since you were "born again." What part of your old life has no place in your new life?

_____

_____

_____

_____

_____

When you pray, commit yourself to living your life differently than you did before you became a Christian. Ask God to teach you how to live as one of His children.

Chapter Four

Do You Know Whom You Are Talking To?

Read ...

If you were to visit five different churches, you probably would see people worship God in five different ways. You might begin to wonder, "Is one way better than another?"

In this chapter, a woman asks Jesus a question like that. She wants to know who worships better—Jews or Samaritans? Jesus listens to the woman and responds by teaching her what worship is all about. As you read, see if you can figure out the proper way to worship God.

John◦Chapter 4

Jesus* learned that the Pharisees had heard, "Jesus is baptizing and making more disciples than John" ²(though Jesus himself didn't baptize them—his disciples did). ³So he left Judea to return to Galilee.

⁴He had to go through Samaria on the way. ⁵Eventually he came to the Samaritan village of Sychar, near the parcel of ground that Jacob gave to his son Joseph. ⁶Jacob's well was there; and Jesus, tired from the long walk, sat wearily beside the well about

4:1 Some manuscripts read *The Lord.*

noontime. [7]Soon a Samaritan woman came to draw water, and Jesus said to her, "Please give me a drink." [8]He was alone at the time because his disciples had gone into the village to buy some food.

[9]The woman was surprised, for Jews refuse to have anything to do with Samaritans. She said to Jesus, "You are a Jew, and I am a Samaritan woman. Why are you asking me for a drink?"

[10]Jesus replied, "If you only knew the gift God has for you and who I am, you would ask me, and I would give you living water."

[11]"But, sir, you don't have a rope or a bucket," she said, "and this is a very deep well. Where would you get this living water? [12]And besides, are you greater than our ancestor Jacob who gave us this well? How can you offer better water than he and his sons and his cattle enjoyed?"

[13]Jesus replied, "People soon become thirsty again after drinking this water. [14]But the water I give them takes away thirst altogether. It becomes a perpetual spring within them, giving them eternal life."

[15]"Please, sir," the woman said, "give me some of that water! Then I'll never be thirsty again, and I won't have to come here to haul water."

[16]"Go and get your husband," Jesus told her.

[17]"I don't have a husband," the woman replied.

Jesus said, "You're right! You don't have a husband—[18]for you have had five husbands, and you aren't even married to the man you're living with now."

[19]"Sir," the woman said, "you must be a prophet. [20]So tell me, why is it that you Jews insist that Jerusalem is the only place of worship, while we Samaritans claim it is here at Mount Gerizim,* where our ancestors worshiped?"

[21]Jesus replied, "Believe me, the time is coming when it will no longer matter whether you worship the Father here or in Jerusalem. [22]You Samaritans know so little about the one you worship, while we Jews know all about him, for salvation comes through the Jews. [23]But the time is coming and is already here when true worshipers will worship the Father in spirit and in

4:20 Greek *on this mountain.*

truth. The Father is looking for anyone who will worship him that way. [24]For God is Spirit, so those who worship him must worship in spirit and in truth."

[25]The woman said, "I know the Messiah will come—the one who is called Christ. When he comes, he will explain everything to us."

[26]Then Jesus told her, "I am the Messiah!"*

[27]Just then his disciples arrived. They were astonished to find him talking to a woman, but none of them asked him why he was doing it or what they had been discussing. [28]The woman left her water jar beside the well and went back to the village and told everyone, [29]"Come and meet a man who told me everything I ever did! Can this be the Messiah?" [30]So the people came streaming from the village to see him.

[31]Meanwhile, the disciples were urging Jesus to eat. [32]"No," he said, "I have food you don't know about."

[33]"Who brought it to him?" the disciples asked each other.

[34]Then Jesus explained: "My nourishment comes from doing the will of God, who sent me, and from finishing his work. [35]Do you think the work of harvesting will not begin until the summer ends four months from now? Look around you! Vast fields are ripening all around us and are ready now for the harvest. [36]The harvesters are paid good wages, and the fruit they harvest is people brought to eternal life. What joy awaits both the planter and the harvester alike! [37]You know the saying, 'One person plants and someone else harvests.' And it's true. [38]I sent you to harvest where you didn't plant; others had already done the work, and you will gather the harvest."

[39]Many Samaritans from the village believed in Jesus because the woman had said, "He told me everything I ever did!" [40]When they came out to see him, they begged him to stay at their village. So he stayed for two days, [41]long enough for many of them to hear his message and believe. [42]Then they said to the woman, "Now we believe because we have heard him ourselves, not just because of what you told us. He is indeed the Savior of the world."

[43]At the end of the two days' stay, Jesus went on into Galilee.

4:26 Greek *"I am, the one speaking to you."*

[44]He had previously said, "A prophet is honored everywhere except in his own country." [45]The Galileans welcomed him, for they had been in Jerusalem at the Passover celebration and had seen all his miraculous signs.

[46]In the course of his journey through Galilee, he arrived at the town of Cana, where he had turned the water into wine. There was a government official in the city of Capernaum whose son was very sick. [47]When he heard that Jesus had come from Judea and was traveling in Galilee, he went over to Cana. He found Jesus and begged him to come to Capernaum with him to heal his son, who was about to die.

[48]Jesus asked, "Must I do miraculous signs and wonders before you people will believe in me?"

[49]The official pleaded, "Lord, please come now before my little boy dies."

[50]Then Jesus told him, "Go back home. Your son will live!" And the man believed Jesus' word and started home.

[51]While he was on his way, some of his servants met him with the news that his son was alive and well. [52]He asked them when the boy had begun to feel better, and they replied, "Yesterday afternoon at one o'clock his fever suddenly disappeared!" [53]Then the father realized it was the same time that Jesus had told him, "Your son will live." And the officer and his entire household believed in Jesus. [54]This was Jesus' second miraculous sign in Galilee after coming from Judea.

Reflect ...

Jesus taught the woman at the well to worship God in spirit and in truth. To worship God is to give a response of respect when the true nature of God is revealed.

In other words, your worship must be led and guided by the Spirit of God. It is not calculated or programmed. Worship is anchored in the truth, the Word of God. It is an honest, gut-level response that comes from the heart. This response can be in the form of a prayer, an act of obedience, or confession of sin.

When you want to worship, it doesn't matter where you are or when you do it. What matters is that you honestly allow the Spirit of God (the Holy Spirit) to lead you and teach you, and that you allow God's Word (the Bible) to guide you and instruct you in the truth.

Respond ...

You can worship God at any time. Write down a time and place when you will worship God in spirit and in truth.

_____

_____

_____

_____

_____

_____

When you pray, ask God to help you learn how to worship better and more often.

Chapter Five

Excuses, Excuses

Read ...

Can you imagine what it would be like to lie on your back, crippled and unable to walk, for thirty-eight years? Maybe you would give up all hope of being healed. Maybe you would keep trying to find something or someone who could heal you or enable you to walk again.

In this chapter, you'll read about a man who still had hope, even after thirty-eight years. He was beside a healing pool, waiting for his turn to get into the healing water. Jesus was known far and wide as a healer and a miracle-worker by the time He arrived at the pool. He stands over the lame man and asks, "Do you want to get well?" You would have thought that the man would have been excited and eager to be healed—but he wasn't. Maybe he was a little bit skeptical or perhaps a little bit frightened. After all, he had grown rather comfortable with his crippled life.

Do you know people like that? People who are afraid to get well? What was this man's response when Jesus asked him if he wanted to get well? Read ahead and find out.

John•Chapter 5

Afterward Jesus returned to Jerusalem for one of the Jewish holy days. ²Inside the city, near the Sheep Gate, was the pool of

Bethesda,* with five covered porches. ³Crowds of sick people—blind, lame, or paralyzed—lay on the porches.* ⁵One of the men lying there had been sick for thirty-eight years. ⁶When Jesus saw him and knew how long he had been ill, he asked him, "Would you like to get well?"

⁷"I can't, sir," the sick man said, "for I have no one to help me into the pool when the water is stirred up. While I am trying to get there, someone else always gets in ahead of me."

⁸Jesus told him, "Stand up, pick up your sleeping mat, and walk!"

⁹Instantly, the man was healed! He rolled up the mat and began walking! But this miracle happened on the Sabbath day. ¹⁰So the Jewish leaders objected. They said to the man who was cured, "You can't work on the Sabbath! It's illegal to carry that sleeping mat!"

¹¹He replied, "The man who healed me said to me, 'Pick up your sleeping mat and walk.' "

¹²"Who said such a thing as that?" they demanded.

¹³The man didn't know, for Jesus had disappeared into the crowd. ¹⁴But afterward Jesus found him in the Temple and told him, "Now you are well; so stop sinning, or something even worse may happen to you." ¹⁵Then the man went to find the Jewish leaders and told them it was Jesus who had healed him.

¹⁶So the Jewish leaders began harassing Jesus for breaking the Sabbath rules. ¹⁷But Jesus replied, "My Father never stops working, so why should I?" ¹⁸So the Jewish leaders tried all the more to kill him. In addition to disobeying the Sabbath rules, he had spoken of God as his Father, thereby making himself equal with God.

¹⁹Jesus replied, "I assure you, the Son can do nothing by himself. He does only what he sees the Father doing. Whatever the Father does, the Son also does. ²⁰For the Father loves the Son and tells him everything he is doing, and the Son will do far greater things than healing this man. You will be astonished at what he does. ²¹He will even raise from the dead anyone he wants to, just

---

5:2 Some manuscripts read *Beth-zatha;* other manuscripts read *Bethsaida.* 5:3 Some manuscripts add *waiting for a certain movement of the water,* ⁴*for an angel of the Lord came from time to time and stirred up the water. And the first person to step down into it afterward was healed.*

as the Father does. ²²And the Father leaves all judgment to his Son, ²³so that everyone will honor the Son, just as they honor the Father. But if you refuse to honor the Son, then you are certainly not honoring the Father who sent him.

²⁴"I assure you, those who listen to my message and believe in God who sent me have eternal life. They will never be condemned for their sins, but they have already passed from death into life.

²⁵"And I assure you that the time is coming, in fact it is here, when the dead will hear my voice—the voice of the Son of God. And those who listen will live. ²⁶The Father has life in himself, and he has granted his Son to have life in himself. ²⁷And he has given him authority to judge all mankind because he is the Son of Man. ²⁸Don't be so surprised! Indeed, the time is coming when all the dead in their graves will hear the voice of God's Son, ²⁹and they will rise again. Those who have done good will rise to eternal life, and those who have continued in evil will rise to judgment. ³⁰But I do nothing without consulting the Father. I judge as I am told. And my judgment is absolutely just, because it is according to the will of God who sent me; it is not merely my own.

³¹"If I were to testify on my own behalf, my testimony would not be valid. ³²But someone else is also testifying about me, and I can assure you that everything he says about me is true. ³³In fact, you sent messengers to listen to John the Baptist, and he preached the truth. ³⁴But the best testimony about me is not from a man, though I have reminded you about John's testimony so you might be saved. ³⁵John shone brightly for a while, and you benefited and rejoiced. ³⁶But I have a greater witness than John—my teachings and my miracles. They have been assigned to me by the Father, and they testify that the Father has sent me. ³⁷And the Father himself has also testified about me. You have never heard his voice or seen him face to face, ³⁸and you do not have his message in your hearts, because you do not believe me—the one he sent to you.

³⁹"You search the Scriptures because you believe they give you eternal life. But the Scriptures point to me! ⁴⁰Yet you refuse to come to me so that I can give you this eternal life.

⁴¹"Your approval or disapproval means nothing to me,

[42]because I know you don't have God's love within you. [43]For I have come to you representing my Father, and you refuse to welcome me, even though you readily accept others who represent only themselves. [44]No wonder you can't believe! For you gladly honor each other, but you don't care about the honor that comes from God alone.

[45]"Yet it is not I who will accuse you of this before the Father. Moses will accuse you! Yes, Moses, on whom you set your hopes. [46]But if you had believed Moses, you would have believed me because he wrote about me. [47]And since you don't believe what he wrote, how will you believe what I say?"

Reflect ...

Did you read about the man beside the pool? Can you believe this guy? Jesus asked him if he wanted to get well and you would expect him to say, "Yes!" Instead, he starts making excuses for why he is crippled. He blames somebody else: "There is no one to help me," he says.

When Jesus asks, "Do you want to get well?" He doesn't want to hear excuses about how messed up your family is. He doesn't want to hear excuses about how life has dealt you a rotten hand or the bad luck you always have. All He wants to know is, "Do you want to get well?"

How would you respond to Jesus if He offered to take away some of your bad habits, a bad relationship, or a bad sin? What was the last excuse you gave God when He wanted to change your life for the better?

Respond ...

Write down one or two excuses that you give for not allowing Jesus to perform miracles in your life.

_____

_____

_____

_____

_____

_____

    When you pray, ask Jesus to touch your life and to heal you of anything that cripples your faith. Let Him know that you are eager and willing to change right now.

Chapter Six

Scaredy Cat!

Read ...

Have you ever been in a situation where you needed help but no one was available to help you? When something like that happens, it's normal to panic, to feel afraid, or to feel hopeless.

In this chapter, the twelve disciples of Jesus were in such a situation. They were out in a boat, in the middle of nowhere, in trouble, and without anyone to help them.

Suddenly Jesus showed up—miraculously. There He was, standing on the water! The disciples didn't smile and say, "Hey, look! Jesus has come to help us. Everything's going to be okay now!" No . . . they had a little different reaction.

Read to find out what happened that day on the Sea of Galilee.

John●Chapter 6

After this, Jesus crossed over the Sea of Galilee, also known as the Sea of Tiberias. ²And a huge crowd kept following him wherever he went, because they saw his miracles as he healed the sick. ³Then Jesus went up into the hills and sat down with his disciples around him. ⁴(It was nearly time for the annual Passover celebration.) ⁵Jesus soon saw a great crowd of people climbing the hill, looking for him. Turning to Philip, he asked, "Philip, where can we buy bread to feed all these people?" [6]He was testing Philip, for he already knew what he was going to do.

[7]Philip replied, "It would take a small fortune* to feed them!"

[8]Then Andrew, Simon Peter's brother, spoke up. [9]"There's a young boy here with five barley loaves and two fish. But what good is that with this huge crowd?"

[10]"Tell everyone to sit down," Jesus ordered. So all of them—the men alone numbered five thousand—sat down on the grassy slopes. [11]Then Jesus took the loaves, gave thanks to God, and passed them out to the people. Afterward he did the same with the fish. And they all ate until they were full. [12]"Now gather the leftovers," Jesus told his disciples, "so that nothing is wasted." [13]There were only five barley loaves to start with, but twelve baskets were filled with the pieces of bread the people did not eat!

[14]When the people saw this miraculous sign, they exclaimed, "Surely, he is the Prophet* we have been expecting!" [15]Jesus saw that they were ready to take him by force and make him king, so he went higher into the hills alone.

[16]That evening his disciples went down to the shore to wait for him. [17]But as darkness fell and Jesus still hadn't come back, they got into the boat and headed out across the lake toward Capernaum. [18]Soon a gale swept down upon them as they rowed, and the sea grew very rough. [19]They were three or four miles* out when suddenly they saw Jesus walking on the water toward the boat. They were terrified, [20]but he called out to them, "I am here! Don't be afraid." [21]Then they were eager to let him in, and immediately the boat arrived at their destination!

[22]The next morning, back across the lake, crowds began gathering on the shore, waiting to see Jesus. For they knew that he and his disciples had come over together and that the disciples had gone off in their boat, leaving him behind. [23]Several boats from Tiberias landed near the place where the Lord had blessed the bread and the people had eaten. [24]When the crowd saw that Jesus wasn't there, nor his disciples, they got into the boats and went across to Capernaum to look for him. [25]When they arrived

6:7 Greek *200 denarii*. A denarius was the equivalent of a full day's wage. **6:14** See Deut 18:15, 18. **6:19** Greek *25 or 30 stadia* [4.6 or 5.5 kilometers].

and found him, they asked, "Teacher, how did you get here?"

²⁶Jesus replied, "The truth is, you want to be with me because I fed you, not because you saw the miraculous sign. ²⁷But you shouldn't be so concerned about perishable things like food. Spend your energy seeking the eternal life that I, the Son of Man, can give you. For God the Father has sent me for that very purpose."

²⁸They replied, "What does God want us to do?"

²⁹Jesus told them, "This is what God wants you to do: Believe in the one he has sent."

³⁰They replied, "You must show us a miraculous sign if you want us to believe in you. What will you do for us? ³¹After all, our ancestors ate manna while they journeyed through the wilderness! As the Scriptures say, 'Moses gave them bread from heaven to eat.'* "

³²Jesus said, "I assure you, Moses didn't give them bread from heaven. My Father did. And now he offers you the true bread from heaven. ³³The true bread of God is the one who comes down from heaven and gives life to the world."

³⁴"Sir," they said, "give us that bread every day of our lives."

³⁵Jesus replied, "I am the bread of life. No one who comes to me will ever be hungry again. Those who believe in me will never thirst. ³⁶But you haven't believed in me even though you have seen me. ³⁷However, those the Father has given me will come to me, and I will never reject them. ³⁸For I have come down from heaven to do the will of God who sent me, not to do what I want. ³⁹And this is the will of God, that I should not lose even one of all those he has given me, but that I should raise them to eternal life at the last day. ⁴⁰For it is my Father's will that all who see his Son and believe in him should have eternal life—that I should raise them at the last day."

⁴¹Then the people* began to murmur in disagreement because he had said, "I am the bread from heaven." ⁴²They said, "This is Jesus, the son of Joseph. We know his father and mother. How can he say, 'I came down from heaven'?"

⁴³But Jesus replied, "Don't complain about what I said. ⁴⁴For

6:31 Exod 16:4; Ps 78:24.   6:41 Greek *Jewish people;* also in 6:52.

people can't come to me unless the Father who sent me draws them to me, and at the last day I will raise them from the dead. [45]As it is written in the Scriptures, 'They will all be taught by God.'* Everyone who hears and learns from the Father comes to me. [46](Not that anyone has ever seen the Father; only I, who was sent from God, have seen him.)

[47]"I assure you, anyone who believes in me already has eternal life. [48]Yes, I am the bread of life! [49]Your ancestors ate manna in the wilderness, but they all died. [50]However, the bread from heaven gives eternal life to everyone who eats it. [51]I am the living bread that came down out of heaven. Anyone who eats this bread will live forever; this bread is my flesh, offered so the world may live."

[52]Then the people began arguing with each other about what he meant. "How can this man give us his flesh to eat?" they asked.

[53]So Jesus said again, "I assure you, unless you eat the flesh of the Son of Man and drink his blood, you cannot have eternal life within you. [54]But those who eat my flesh and drink my blood have eternal life, and I will raise them at the last day. [55]For my flesh is the true food, and my blood is the true drink. [56]All who eat my flesh and drink my blood remain in me, and I in them. [57]I live by the power of the living Father who sent me; in the same way, those who partake of me will live because of me. [58]I am the true bread from heaven. Anyone who eats this bread will live forever and not die as your ancestors did, even though they ate the manna."

[59]He said these things while he was teaching in the synagogue in Capernaum.

[60]Even his disciples said, "This is very hard to understand. How can anyone accept it?"

[61]Jesus knew within himself that his disciples were complaining, so he said to them, "Does this offend you? [62]Then what will you think if you see me, the Son of Man, return to heaven again? [63]It is the Spirit who gives eternal life. Human effort accomplishes nothing. And the very words I have spoken to you are spirit and life. [64]But some of you don't believe me." (For Jesus knew from the beginning who didn't believe, and he knew who would betray

6:45 Isa 54:13.

him.) [65]Then he said, "That is what I meant when I said that people can't come to me unless the Father brings them to me."

[66]At this point many of his disciples turned away and deserted him. [67]Then Jesus turned to the Twelve and asked, "Are you going to leave, too?"

[68]Simon Peter replied, "Lord, to whom would we go? You alone have the words that give eternal life. [69]We believe them, and we know you are the Holy One of God."

[70]Then Jesus said, "I chose the twelve of you, but one is a devil." [71]He was speaking of Judas, son of Simon Iscariot, one of the Twelve, who would betray him.

Reflect ...

Isn't it interesting that the disciples were afraid when Jesus came to them on the Sea of Galilee? John doesn't go into detail, but chances are they screamed in fright, "Look out! There's a ghost on the water!"

But Jesus calmed them down: "Don't be afraid. It's me, Jesus."

Are there times when you feel afraid? You can be assured that Jesus is with you—always (Matthew 28:20). And when Jesus is around, there is no need for fear.

Respond ...

In the space below, describe a situation that sometimes causes you to experience fear. Then write the words of Jesus in verse 20 three times.

_____

_____

_____

_____

_____

_____

When you pray, ask God to take away your fear and to re-
place it with complete faith and trust in Jesus.

• Chapter Seven •

Not Yet

Read ...

Many people think that Jesus' ministry was a huge success story: incredible sermons, impressive miracles, and huge crowds. They think everywhere Jesus went, people wanted autographs and were ready to follow Him anywhere.

But that wasn't true at all. Even though Jesus loved people and helped people, His life was constantly being threatened by others. There were many people out to discredit Him and even kill Him.

Jesus stayed focused on what He was called to do. Despite opposition, He was confident and He overcame fear.

Focus your reading on verses 1–31 and find the two verses that describe the key to Jesus' confidence in the face of adversity.

John • Chapter 7

After this, Jesus stayed in Galilee, going from village to village. He wanted to stay out of Judea where the Jewish leaders were plotting his death. ²But soon it was time for the Festival of Shelters, ³and Jesus' brothers urged him to go to Judea for the celebration. "Go where your followers can see your miracles!" they scoffed. ⁴"You can't become a public figure if you hide like this! If you can do such wonderful things, prove it to the world!" ⁵For even his brothers didn't believe in him.

⁶Jesus replied, "Now is not the right time for me to go. But you can go anytime, and it will make no difference. ⁷The world can't hate you, but it does hate me because I accuse it of sin and evil. ⁸You go on. I am not yet* ready to go to this festival, because my time has not yet come." ⁹So Jesus remained in Galilee.

¹⁰But after his brothers had left for the festival, Jesus also went, though secretly, staying out of public view. ¹¹The Jewish leaders tried to find him at the festival and kept asking if anyone had seen him. ¹²There was a lot of discussion about him among the crowds. Some said, "He's a wonderful man," while others said, "He's nothing but a fraud, deceiving the people." ¹³But no one had the courage to speak favorably about him in public, for they were afraid of getting in trouble with the Jewish leaders.

¹⁴Then, midway through the festival, Jesus went up to the Temple and began to teach. ¹⁵The Jewish leaders were surprised when they heard him. "How does he know so much when he hasn't studied everything we've studied?" they asked.

¹⁶So Jesus told them, "I'm not teaching my own ideas, but those of God who sent me. ¹⁷Anyone who wants to do the will of God will know whether my teaching is from God or is merely my own. ¹⁸Those who present their own ideas are looking for praise for themselves, but those who seek to honor the one who sent them are good and genuine. ¹⁹None of you obeys the law of Moses! In fact, you are trying to kill me."

²⁰The crowd replied, "You're demon possessed! Who's trying to kill you?"

²¹Jesus replied, "I worked on the Sabbath by healing a man, and you were offended. ²²But you work on the Sabbath, too, when you obey Moses' law of circumcision. (Actually, this tradition of circumcision is older than the law of Moses; it goes back to Abraham.) ²³For if the correct time for circumcising your son falls on the Sabbath, you go ahead and do it, so as not to break the law of Moses. So why should I be condemned for making a man completely well on the Sabbath? ²⁴Think this through and you will see that I am right."

7:8 Some manuscripts omit *yet.*

²⁵Some of the people who lived there in Jerusalem said among themselves, "Isn't this the man they are trying to kill? ²⁶But here he is, speaking in public, and they say nothing to him. Can it be that our leaders know that he really is the Messiah? ²⁷But how could he be? For we know where this man comes from. When the Messiah comes, he will simply appear; no one will know where he comes from."

²⁸While Jesus was teaching in the Temple, he called out, "Yes, you know me, and you know where I come from. But I represent one you don't know, and he is true. ²⁹I know him beca⁻se I have come from him, and he sent me to you." ³⁰Then the leaders tried to arrest him; but no one laid a hand on him, because his time had not yet come.

³¹Many among the crowds at the Temple believed in him. "After all," they said, "would you expect the Messiah to do more miraculous signs than this man has done?"

³²When the Pharisees heard that the crowds were murmuring such things, they and the leading priests sent Temple guards to arrest Jesus. ³³But Jesus told them, "I will be here a little longer. Then I will return to the one who sent me. ³⁴You will search for me but not find me. And you won't be able to come where I am."

³⁵The Jewish leaders were puzzled by this statement. "Where is he planning to go?" they asked. "Maybe he is thinking of leaving the country and going to the Jews in other lands, or maybe even to the Gentiles! ³⁶What does he mean when he says, 'You will search for me but not find me,' and 'You won't be able to come where I am'?"

³⁷On the last day, the climax of the festival, Jesus stood and shouted to the crowds, "If you are thirsty, come to me! ³⁸If you believe in me, come and drink! For the Scriptures declare that rivers of living water will flow out from within."* ³⁹(When he said "living water," he was speaking of the Spirit, who would be given to everyone believing in him. But the Spirit had not yet been given, because Jesus had not yet entered into his glory.)

⁴⁰When the crowds heard him say this, some of them declared,

7:37-38 Or *"Let anyone who is thirsty come to me and drink.* ³⁸*For the Scriptures declare that rivers of living water will flow from the heart of those who believe in me."*

"This man surely is the Prophet."* [41]Others said, "He is the Messiah." Still others said, "But he can't be! Will the Messiah come from Galilee? [42]For the Scriptures clearly state that the Messiah will be born of the royal line of David, in Bethlehem, the village where King David was born."* [43]So the crowd was divided in their opinion about him. [44]And some wanted him arrested, but no one touched him.

[45]The Temple guards who had been sent to arrest him returned to the leading priests and Pharisees. "Why didn't you bring him in?" they demanded.

[46]"We have never heard anyone talk like this!" the guards responded.

[47]"Have you been led astray, too?" the Pharisees mocked. [48]"Is there a single one of us rulers or Pharisees who believes in him? [49]These ignorant crowds do, but what do they know about it? A curse on them anyway!"

[50]Nicodemus, the leader who had met with Jesus earlier, then spoke up. [51]"Is it legal to convict a man before he is given a hearing?" he asked.

[52]They replied, "Are you from Galilee, too? Search the Scriptures and see for yourself—no prophet ever comes from Galilee!"

The most ancient Greek manuscripts do not include John 7:53–8:11.

[53]Then the meeting broke up and everybody went home.

Reflect ...

On two separate occasions (verse 8 and 30), Scripture stated that it was not yet Jesus' time. He knew that no one could disrupt God's plan, no matter what power they claimed to have. He also knew that when His time came (to die on the cross), there was nothing that anyone on earth could do about it. Jesus did not live according to what the world said would happen, but according to what God said would happen.

7:40 See Deut 18:15, 18.   **7:42** See Mic 5:2.

In the same way, you don't live by what the world says, but by what God says.

If God wants you to live for Christ, do it without compromise. If He wants you to pray, teach, or share Christ with others, do it without fear. Don't be concerned with how people treat you. People can only hurt you temporarily. Be more concerned about your relationship with God. God gives you eternal life.

Respond ...

Write down the three worst things that could happen to you if you were to obey God in front of your friends and family. Would you be willing to accept these in exchange for a close relationship with God?

_____

_____

_____

_____

_____

When you pray, ask God to give you complete confidence in Him.

Guess what! You are one-third of the way through your 21 Jump-Start Program.

• Chapter Eight •

Busted, Then Trusted

Read ...

Can you imagine living in a country where sex outside of marriage was punishable by death?

Well, in Jesus' day, that was the law. Mess around with someone you aren't married to—and you die.

In this chapter, a woman was caught in the act of adultery. A group of men, knowing that this woman by law should be put to death immediately, asked Jesus what He would do.

What do you think He did? Focus your reading on verses 1–11 and you'll find out.

John●Chapter 8

Jesus returned to the Mount of Olives, ²but early the next morning he was back again at the Temple. A crowd soon gathered, and he sat down and taught them. ³As he was speaking, the teachers of religious law and Pharisees brought a woman they had caught in the act of adultery. They put her in front of the crowd.

⁴"Teacher," they said to Jesus, "this woman was caught in the very act of adultery. ⁵The law of Moses says to stone her. What do you say?"

⁶They were trying to trap him into saying something they could use against him, but Jesus stooped down and wrote in the dust with his finger. ⁷They kept demanding an answer, so he stood

up again and said, "All right, stone her. But let those who have never sinned throw the first stones!" ⁸Then he stooped down again and wrote in the dust.

⁹When the accusers heard this, they slipped away one by one, beginning with the oldest, until only Jesus was left in the middle of the crowd with the woman. ¹⁰Then Jesus stood up again and said to her, "Where are your accusers? Didn't even one of them condemn you?"

¹¹"No, Lord," she said.

And Jesus said, "Neither do I. Go and sin no more."

¹²Jesus said to the people, "I am the light of the world. If you follow me, you won't be stumbling through the darkness, because you will have the light that leads to life."

¹³The Pharisees replied, "You are making false claims about yourself!"

¹⁴Jesus told them, "These claims are valid even though I make them about myself. For I know where I came from and where I am going, but you don't know this about me. ¹⁵You judge me with all your human limitations,* but I am not judging anyone. ¹⁶And if I did, my judgment would be correct in every respect because I am not alone—I have with me the Father who sent me. ¹⁷Your own law says that if two people agree about something, their witness is accepted as fact.* ¹⁸I am one witness, and my Father who sent me is the other."

¹⁹"Where is your father?" they asked.

Jesus answered, "Since you don't know who I am, you don't know who my Father is. If you knew me, then you would know my Father, too." ²⁰Jesus made these statements while he was teaching in the section of the Temple known as the Treasury. But he was not arrested, because his time had not yet come.

²¹Later Jesus said to them again, "I am going away. You will search for me and die in your sin. You cannot come where I am going."

²²The Jewish leaders asked, "Is he planning to commit suicide? What does he mean, 'You cannot come where I am going'?"

²³Then he said to them, "You are from below; I am from above.

8:15 Or *judge me by human standards.* **8:17** See Deut 19:15.

You are of this world; I am not. ²⁴That is why I said that you will die in your sins; for unless you believe that I am who I say I am, you will die in your sins."

²⁵"Tell us who you are," they demanded.

Jesus replied, "I am the one I have always claimed to be.* ²⁶I have much to say about you and much to condemn, but I won't. For I say only what I have heard from the one who sent me, and he is true." ²⁷But they still didn't understand that he was talking to them about his Father.

²⁸So Jesus said, "When you have lifted up the Son of Man on the cross, then you will realize that I am he and that I do nothing on my own, but I speak what the Father taught me. ²⁹And the one who sent me is with me—he has not deserted me. For I always do those things that are pleasing to him." ³⁰Then many who heard him say these things believed in him.

³¹Jesus said to the people* who believed in him, "You are truly my disciples if you keep obeying my teachings. ³²And you will know the truth, and the truth will set you free."

³³"But we are descendants of Abraham," they said. "We have never been slaves to anyone on earth. What do you mean, 'set free'?"

³⁴Jesus replied, "I assure you that everyone who sins is a slave of sin. ³⁵A slave is not a permanent member of the family, but a son is part of the family forever. ³⁶So if the Son sets you free, you will indeed be free. ³⁷Yes, I realize that you are descendants of Abraham. And yet some of you are trying to kill me because my message does not find a place in your hearts. ³⁸I am telling you what I saw when I was with my Father. But you are following the advice of your father."

³⁹"Our father is Abraham," they declared.

"No," Jesus replied, "for if you were children of Abraham, you would follow his good example.* ⁴⁰I told you the truth I heard from God, but you are trying to kill me. Abraham wouldn't do a thing like that. ⁴¹No, you are obeying your real father when you act that way."

8:25 Or *"Why do I speak to you at all?"* 8:31 Greek *Jewish people;* also in 8:48, 52, 57. 8:39 Some manuscripts read *if you are children of Abraham, follow his example.*

They replied, "We were not born out of wedlock! Our true Father is God himself."

[42]Jesus told them, "If God were your Father, you would love me, because I have come to you from God. I am not here on my own, but he sent me. [43]Why can't you understand what I am saying? It is because you are unable to do so! [44]For you are the children of your father the Devil, and you love to do the evil things he does. He was a murderer from the beginning and has always hated the truth. There is no truth in him. When he lies, it is consistent with his character; for he is a liar and the father of lies. [45]So when I tell the truth, you just naturally don't believe me! [46]Which of you can truthfully accuse me of sin? And since I am telling you the truth, why don't you believe me? [47]Anyone whose Father is God listens gladly to the words of God. Since you don't, it proves you aren't God's children."

[48]The people retorted, "You Samaritan devil! Didn't we say all along that you were possessed by a demon?"

[49]"No," Jesus said, "I have no demon in me. For I honor my Father—and you dishonor me. [50]And though I have no wish to glorify myself, God wants to glorify me. Let him be the judge. [51]I assure you, anyone who obeys my teaching will never die!"

[52]The people said, "Now we know you are possessed by a demon. Even Abraham and the prophets died, but you say that those who obey your teaching will never die! [53]Are you greater than our father Abraham, who died? Are you greater than the prophets, who died? Who do you think you are?"

[54]Jesus answered, "If I am merely boasting about myself, it doesn't count. But it is my Father who says these glorious things about me. You say, 'He is our God,' [55]but you do not even know him. I know him. If I said otherwise, I would be as great a liar as you! But it is true—I know him and obey him. [56]Your ancestor Abraham rejoiced as he looked forward to my coming. He saw it and was glad."

[57]The people said, "You aren't even fifty years old. How can you say you have seen Abraham?*"

8:57 Some manuscripts read *How can you say Abraham has seen you?* 8:58 Or *"Truly, truly, before Abraham was, I am."*

[58]Jesus answered, "The truth is, I existed before Abraham was even born!"* [59]At that point they picked up stones to kill him. But Jesus hid himself from them and left the Temple.

Reflect ...

What did Jesus do when the adulterous woman was brought to Him? As you read, Jesus forgave her and sent her on her way with one piece of advice: "Sin no more." She was busted, then trusted with freedom.

All of us were busted for sin and then trusted with freedom. You were given freedom—not only from the penalty of sin (death), but the power of sin. Sin does not have to control you any longer. Just like He did for the woman, Jesus has given us a commandment to "sin no more." He would never ask you to do something you couldn't do. Sin has no control over you, but Jesus does. He will help you to resist temptation and to *say no* to a life of sin.

Respond ...

In the space below, write down these three things:

1. A sin in your life that you struggle with.

2. A person you know who might be able to help you overcome this sin—someone who will pray for you and hold you accountable.

3. One action you can take to help you avoid the temptation to commit this sin.

_____

_____

_____

_____

_____

_____

   When you pray, ask God to give you the strength to overcome sin in your life.

• Chapter Nine •

Spiritually Challenged?

Read ...

Everyone has a handicap of some sort. We all know people who have severe handicaps, such as the inability to walk or speak. Sometimes we use politically correct terms like "visually challenged" (for blindness) or "audibly challenged" (for deafness). Some handicaps are not so noticeable. Some folks are musically challenged (tone deaf), athletically challenged (uncoordinated), or vertically challenged (short). What is your handicap?

We often wonder why individuals have handicaps. Did they do something wrong? Are they being punished for something they did—or something their parents did?

The answer to the questions, according to the Bible, is no.

God doesn't blame us or anyone else for our handicaps. He wants to use our handicaps and be glorified in them. Focus your reading on verses 1–41 and find out more.

John•Chapter 9

As Jesus was walking along, he saw a man who had been blind from birth. ²"Teacher," his disciples asked him, "why was this man born blind? Was it a result of his own sins or those of his parents?"

³"It was not because of his sins or his parents' sins," Jesus an-

swered. "He was born blind so the power of God could be seen in him. ⁴All of us must quickly carry out the tasks assigned us by the one who sent me, because there is little time left before the night falls and all work comes to an end. ⁵But while I am still here in the world, I am the light of the world."

⁶Then he spit on the ground, made mud with the saliva, and smoothed the mud over the blind man's eyes. ⁷He told him, "Go and wash in the pool of Siloam" (Siloam means Sent). So the man went and washed, and came back seeing!

⁸His neighbors and others who knew him as a blind beggar asked each other, "Is this the same man—that beggar?" ⁹Some said he was, and others said, "No, but he surely looks like him!"

And the beggar kept saying, "I am the same man!"

¹⁰They asked, "Who healed you? What happened?"

¹¹He told them, "The man they call Jesus made mud and smoothed it over my eyes and told me, 'Go to the pool of Siloam and wash off the mud.' I went and washed, and now I can see!"

¹²"Where is he now?" they asked.

"I don't know," he replied.

¹³Then they took the man to the Pharisees. ¹⁴Now as it happened, Jesus had healed the man on a Sabbath. ¹⁵The Pharisees asked the man all about it. So he told them, "He smoothed the mud over my eyes, and when it was washed away, I could see!"

¹⁶Some of the Pharisees said, "This man Jesus is not from God, for he is working on the Sabbath." Others said, "But how could an ordinary sinner do such miraculous signs?" So there was a deep division of opinion among them.

¹⁷Then the Pharisees once again questioned the man who had been blind and demanded, "This man who opened your eyes— who do you say he is?"

The man replied, "I think he must be a prophet."

¹⁸The Jewish leaders wouldn't believe he had been blind, so they called in his parents. ¹⁹They asked them, "Is this your son? Was he born blind? If so, how can he see?"

²⁰His parents replied, "We know this is our son and that he was born blind, ²¹but we don't know how he can see or who healed him. He is old enough to speak for himself. Ask him."

²²They said this because they were afraid of the Jewish leaders, who had announced that anyone saying Jesus was the Messiah would be expelled from the synagogue. ²³That's why they said, "He is old enough to speak for himself. Ask him."

²⁴So for the second time they called in the man who had been blind and told him, "Give glory to God by telling the truth,* because we know Jesus is a sinner."

²⁵"I don't know whether he is a sinner," the man replied. "But I know this: I was blind, and now I can see!"

²⁶"But what did he do?" they asked. "How did he heal you?"

²⁷"Look!" the man exclaimed. "I told you once. Didn't you listen? Why do you want to hear it again? Do you want to become his disciples, too?"

²⁸Then they cursed him and said, "You are his disciple, but we are disciples of Moses. ²⁹We know God spoke to Moses, but as for this man, we don't know anything about him."

³⁰"Why, that's very strange!" the man replied. "He healed my eyes, and yet you don't know anything about him! ³¹Well, God doesn't listen to sinners, but he is ready to hear those who worship him and do his will. ³²Never since the world began has anyone been able to open the eyes of someone born blind. ³³If this man were not from God, he couldn't do it."

³⁴"You were born in sin!" they answered. "Are you trying to teach us?" And they threw him out of the synagogue.

³⁵When Jesus heard what had happened, he found the man and said, "Do you believe in the Son of Man*?"

³⁶The man answered, "Who is he, sir, because I would like to."

³⁷"You have seen him," Jesus said, "and he is speaking to you!"

³⁸"Yes, Lord," the man said, "I believe!" And he worshiped Jesus.

³⁹Then Jesus told him, "I have come to judge the world. I have come to give sight to the blind and to show those who think they see that they are blind."

⁴⁰The Pharisees who were standing there heard him and

9:24 Or *Give glory to God, not to Jesus;* Greek reads *Give glory to God.* **9:35** Some manuscripts read *the Son of God.*

asked, "Are you saying we are blind?"

⁴¹"If you were blind, you wouldn't be guilty," Jesus replied. "But you remain guilty because you claim you can see."

Reflect ...

The people who didn't understand the man's blindness in this chapter were handicapped themselves. They were spiritually challenged. They didn't understand God wanted to use this man's handicap to demonstrate His power and glory.

In the same way, all of us were born spiritually challenged. We were born into a life of sin, but God wants to use this handicap to demonstrate His power and glory in our lives.

We have many other weaknesses which God can use to demonstrate His power and glory as well. The apostle Paul even bragged about his weaknesses (his handicaps) because he knew that God would be glorified in them (2 Corinthians 12:9).

What handicap or weakness do you have that God can use? How will you allow Him to use it?

Respond ...

Write down a weakness or handicap you have. Are you willing to give it to God?

_____

_____

_____

_____

_____

When you pray, ask God to use that weakness to bring glory and honor to himself.

• Chapter Ten •

"Scam Artists"

Read ...

Are you familiar with the term "scam artist"? This is a person who will promise you all kinds of stuff in order to get something from you. They might promise you a good time, a better life, more happiness, or something very expensive for free.

But they rarely are able to deliver on their promises. They are only interested in themselves.

Jesus, on the other hand, always makes good on His promises. No one can do for you what Jesus can. His promises are based on His unconditional love for you. Jesus calls scam artists "thieves" and "liars" and declares that they are only working for Satan.

When you read chapter ten, focus on verses 1–10 and compare what Satan has to offer with what Jesus has to offer.

John○Chapter 10

"I assure you, anyone who sneaks over the wall of a sheepfold, rather than going through the gate, must surely be a thief and a robber! ²For a shepherd enters through the gate. ³The gatekeeper opens the gate for him, and the sheep hear his voice and come to him. He calls his own sheep by name and leads them out. ⁴After he has gathered his own flock, he walks ahead of them, and they follow him because they recognize his voice. ⁵They won't follow a stranger; they will run from him because they don't recognize his voice.''

⁶Those who heard Jesus use this illustration didn't understand what he meant, ⁷so he explained it to them. "I assure you, I am the gate for the sheep," he said. ⁸"All others who came before me were thieves and robbers. But the true sheep did not listen to them. ⁹Yes, I am the gate. Those who come in through me will be saved. Wherever they go, they will find green pastures. ¹⁰The thief's purpose is to steal and kill and destroy. My purpose is to give life in all its fullness.

¹¹"I am the good shepherd. The good shepherd lays down his life for the sheep. ¹²A hired hand will run when he sees a wolf coming. He will leave the sheep because they aren't his and he isn't their shepherd. And so the wolf attacks them and scatters the flock. ¹³The hired hand runs away because he is merely hired and has no real concern for the sheep.

¹⁴"I am the good shepherd; I know my own sheep, and they know me, ¹⁵just as my Father knows me and I know the Father. And I lay down my life for the sheep. ¹⁶I have other sheep, too, that are not in this sheepfold. I must bring them also, and they will listen to my voice; and there will be one flock with one shepherd.

¹⁷"The Father loves me because I lay down my life that I may have it back again. ¹⁸No one can take my life from me. I lay down my life voluntarily. For I have the right to lay it down when I want to and also the power to take it again. For my Father has given me this command.''

¹⁹When he said these things, the people* were again divided in their opinions about him. ²⁰Some of them said, "He has a demon, or he's crazy. Why listen to a man like that?" ²¹Others said, "This doesn't sound like a man possessed by a demon! Can a demon open the eyes of the blind?"

²²It was now winter, and Jesus was in Jerusalem at the time of Hanukkah.* ²³He was at the Temple, walking through the section known as Solomon's Colonnade. ²⁴The Jewish leaders surrounded him and asked, "How long are you going to keep us in suspense?

10:19 Greek *Jewish people.* **10:22** Or *the Festival of Dedication.*

If you are the Messiah, tell us plainly."

[25]Jesus replied, "I have already told you, and you don't believe me. The proof is what I do in the name of my Father. [26]But you don't believe me because you are not part of my flock. [27]My sheep recognize my voice; I know them, and they follow me. [28]I give them eternal life, and they will never perish. No one will snatch them away from me, [29]for my Father has given them to me, and he is more powerful than anyone else. So no one can take them from me. [30]The Father and I are one."

[31]Once again the Jewish leaders picked up stones to kill him. [32]Jesus said, "At my Father's direction I have done many things to help the people. For which one of these good deeds are you killing me?"

[33]They replied, "Not for any good work, but for blasphemy, because you, a mere man, have made yourself God."

[34]Jesus replied, "It is written in your own law that God said to certain leaders of the people, 'I say, you are gods!'* [35]And you know that the Scriptures cannot be altered. So if those people, who received God's message, were called 'gods,' [36]why do you call it blasphemy when the Holy One who was sent into the world by the Father says, 'I am the Son of God'? [37]Don't believe me unless I carry out my Father's work. [38]But if I do his work, believe in what I have done, even if you don't believe me. Then you will realize that the Father is in me, and I am in the Father."

[39]Once again they tried to arrest him, but he got away and left them. [40]He went beyond the Jordan River to stay near the place where John was first baptizing. [41]And many followed him. "John didn't do miracles," they remarked to one another, "but all his predictions about this man have come true." [42]And many believed in him there.

Reflect ...

In this chapter, you can see the difference between what Satan offers and what Jesus offers. Jesus promises to give life, but Satan only promises death.

10:34 Ps 82:6.

How do you know which is which? Remember this: Life comes from God's Word, and death comes from scam artists who are working for Satan. They offer a different gospel, one that comes from the world.

Take a personal inventory of your life. What are your hobbies? Who are your friends? How do you spend your free time? Are these activities consistent with what you know God wants you to do? Are they consistent with the Word of God? Are you following the Good Shepherd or a thief and liar?

Respond ...

In the space below, list some of the activities that are most important to you.

_____

_____

_____

_____

_____

When you pray, ask God to help you set priorities for your life that are consistent with what He wants you to do.

Chapter Eleven

Can I Have a Word With You?

Read ...

Have you ever wondered why God does the things He does in the way He does? I sure do. It's okay to ask questions like that, as long as you don't cast judgment on God. God is always right, no matter what He seems to be doing. What we must do is be patient and wait to see what the outcome will be.

In this chapter, we read the story of Lazarus, one of Jesus' best friends. Lazarus is dying. His sisters, Mary and Martha, beg Jesus to come and heal him. But Jesus doesn't go right away and Lazarus dies. Suddenly Jesus is in hot water with Mary and Martha and they jam Him up about it. What do you think Jesus did? Focus your reading on verses 1–44.

John•Chapter 11

A man named Lazarus was sick. He lived in Bethany with his sisters, Mary and Martha. ²This is the Mary who poured the expensive perfume on the Lord's feet and wiped them with her hair.* Her brother, Lazarus, was sick. ³So the two sisters sent a

11:2 This incident is recorded in chapter 12.

message to Jesus telling him, "Lord, the one you love is very sick."

⁴But when Jesus heard about it he said, "Lazarus's sickness will not end in death. No, it is for the glory of God. I, the Son of God, will receive glory from this." ⁵Although Jesus loved Martha, Mary, and Lazarus, ⁶he stayed where he was for the next two days and did not go to them. ⁷Finally after two days, he said to his disciples, "Let's go to Judea again."

⁸But his disciples objected. "Teacher," they said, "only a few days ago the Jewish leaders in Judea were trying to kill you. Are you going there again?"

⁹Jesus replied, "There are twelve hours of daylight every day. As long as it is light, people can walk safely. They can see because they have the light of this world. ¹⁰Only at night is there danger of stumbling because there is no light." ¹¹Then he said, "Our friend Lazarus has fallen asleep, but now I will go and wake him up."

¹²The disciples said, "Lord, if he is sleeping, that means he is getting better!" ¹³They thought Jesus meant Lazarus was having a good night's rest, but Jesus meant Lazarus had died.

¹⁴Then he told them plainly, "Lazarus is dead. ¹⁵And for your sake, I am glad I wasn't there, because this will give you another opportunity to believe in me. Come, let's go see him."

¹⁶Thomas, nicknamed the Twin,* said to his fellow disciples, "Let's go, too—and die with Jesus."

¹⁷When Jesus arrived at Bethany, he was told that Lazarus had already been in his grave for four days. ¹⁸Bethany was only a few miles* down the road from Jerusalem, ¹⁹and many of the people* had come to pay their respects and console Martha and Mary on their loss. ²⁰When Martha got word that Jesus was coming, she went to meet him. But Mary stayed at home. ²¹Martha said to Jesus, "Lord, if you had been here, my brother would not have died. ²²But even now I know that God will give you whatever you ask."

²³Jesus told her, "Your brother will rise again."

11:16 Greek *the one who was called Didymus.* 11:18 Greek *was about 15 stadia* [about 2.8 kilometers]. 11:19 Greek *Jewish people;* also 11:31, 33, 36, 45, 54.

[24]"Yes," Martha said, "when everyone else rises, on resurrection day."

[25]Jesus told her, "I am the resurrection and the life.* Those who believe in me, even though they die like everyone else, will live again. [26]They are given eternal life for believing in me and will never perish. Do you believe this, Martha?"

[27]"Yes, Lord," she told him. "I have always believed you are the Messiah, the Son of God, the one who has come into the world from God." [28]Then she left him and returned to Mary. She called Mary aside from the mourners and told her, "The Teacher is here and wants to see you." [29]So Mary immediately went to him.

[30]Now Jesus had stayed outside the village, at the place where Martha met him. [31]When the people who were at the house trying to console Mary saw her leave so hastily, they assumed she was going to Lazarus's grave to weep. So they followed her there. [32]When Mary arrived and saw Jesus, she fell down at his feet and said, "Lord, if you had been here, my brother would not have died."

[33]When Jesus saw her weeping and saw the other people wailing with her, he was moved with indignation and was deeply troubled. [34]"Where have you put him?" he asked them.

They told him, "Lord, come and see." [35]Then Jesus wept. [36]The people who were standing nearby said, "See how much he loved him." [37]But some said, "This man healed a blind man. Why couldn't he keep Lazarus from dying?"

[38]And again Jesus was deeply troubled. Then they came to the grave. It was a cave with a stone rolled across its entrance. [39]"Roll the stone aside," Jesus told them.

But Martha, the dead man's sister, said, "Lord, by now the smell will be terrible because he has been dead for four days."

[40]Jesus responded, "Didn't I tell you that you will see God's glory if you believe?" [41]So they rolled the stone aside. Then Jesus looked up to heaven and said, "Father, thank you for hearing me. [42]You always hear me, but I said it out loud for the sake of all these people standing here, so they will believe you sent me." [43]Then Jesus shouted, "Lazarus, come out!" [44]And Lazarus came out,

11:25 Some manuscripts do not include *and the life.*

bound in graveclothes, his face wrapped in a headcloth. Jesus told them, "Unwrap him and let him go!"

⁴⁵Many of the people who were with Mary believed in Jesus when they saw this happen. ⁴⁶But some went to the Pharisees and told them what Jesus had done. ⁴⁷Then the leading priests and Pharisees called the high council* together to discuss the situation. "What are we going to do?" they asked each other. "This man certainly performs many miraculous signs. ⁴⁸If we leave him alone, the whole nation will follow him, and then the Roman army will come and destroy both our Temple and our nation."

⁴⁹And one of them, Caiaphas, who was high priest that year, said, "How can you be so stupid? ⁵⁰Why should the whole nation be destroyed? Let this one man die for the people."

⁵¹This prophecy that Jesus should die for the entire nation came from Caiaphas in his position as high priest. He didn't think of it himself; he was inspired to say it. ⁵²It was a prediction that Jesus' death would be not for Israel only, but for the gathering together of all the children of God scattered around the world.

⁵³So from that time on the Jewish leaders began to plot Jesus' death. ⁵⁴As a result, Jesus stopped his public ministry among the people and left Jerusalem. He went to a place near the wilderness, to the village of Ephraim, and stayed there with his disciples.

⁵⁵It was now almost time for the celebration of Passover, and many people from the country arrived in Jerusalem several days early so they could go through the cleansing ceremony before the Passover began. ⁵⁶They wanted to see Jesus, and as they talked in the Temple, they asked each other, "What do you think? Will he come for the Passover?" ⁵⁷Meanwhile, the leading priests and Pharisees had publicly announced that anyone seeing Jesus must report him immediately so they could arrest him.

Reflect ...

When Jesus arrived at the home of Mary and Martha, Lazarus was dead. Things seemed hopeless. But Jesus didn't let

11:47 Greek *the Sanhedrin.*

death have the last word in this situation. He raised Lazarus from the dead by simply calling his name.

All Jesus had to do was speak one word and a miracle took place. Do you realize that you are always one spoken word away from an answer to your problem or the wisdom you need to deal with any situation? Jesus can perform a miracle in your life with one word.

What word from Jesus do you need today?

Respond ...

In the space below, write a problem or situation that you would like Jesus to speak life into today.

_____

_____

_____

_____

_____

_____

When you pray, ask Jesus, by faith, to speak to you and to give you the wisdom and direction you need to deal with the problem you have written about. Ask Him to give you the Word you need.

• Chapter Twelve •

See Any Miracles Lately?

Read ...

Not long after Jesus raised Lazarus from the dead, He went back to Lazarus's house for dinner. Lazarus's two sisters, Mary and Martha, were also there. Mary did something very extravagant to show Jesus how much she loved Him. She poured expensive perfume on His feet and then wiped His feet dry with her hair. Meanwhile, Martha prepared supper. While this was going on in the house, something very interesting was being planned by the religious hypocrites who were watching all this happen. See if you can figure out what it is and how Lazarus got caught in the middle.

John•Chapter 12

Six days before the Passover ceremonies began, Jesus arrived in Bethany, the home of Lazarus—the man he had raised from the dead. ²A dinner was prepared in Jesus' honor. Martha served, and Lazarus sat at the table with him. ³Then Mary took a twelve-ounce jar* of expensive perfume made from essence of nard, and she anointed Jesus' feet with it and wiped his feet with her hair. And the house was filled with fragrance.

⁴But Judas Iscariot, one of his disciples—the one who would

12:3 Greek *took 1 litra* [327 grams].

betray him—said, [5]"That perfume was worth a small fortune.* It should have been sold and the money given to the poor." [6]Not that he cared for the poor—he was a thief who was in charge of the disciples' funds, and he often took some for his own use.

[7]Jesus replied, "Leave her alone. She did it in preparation for my burial. [8]You will always have the poor among you, but I will not be here with you much longer."

[9]When all the people* heard of Jesus' arrival, they flocked to see him and also to see Lazarus, the man Jesus had raised from the dead. [10]Then the leading priests decided to kill Lazarus, too, [11]for it was because of him that many of the people had deserted them and believed in Jesus.

[12]The next day, the news that Jesus was on the way to Jerusalem swept through the city. A huge crowd of Passover visitors [13]took palm branches and went down the road to meet him. They shouted,

"Praise God!*
Bless the one who comes in the name of the Lord!
Hail to the King of Israel!"*

[14]Jesus found a young donkey and sat on it, fulfilling the prophecy that said:

[15] "Don't be afraid, people of Israel.*
Look, your King is coming,
      sitting on a donkey's colt."*

[16]His disciples didn't realize at the time that this was a fulfillment of prophecy. But after Jesus entered into his glory, they remembered that these Scriptures had come true before their eyes.

[17]Those in the crowd who had seen Jesus call Lazarus back to life were telling others all about it. [18]That was the main reason so many went out to meet him—because they had heard about this mighty miracle. [19]Then the Pharisees said to each other, "We've lost. Look, the whole world has gone after him!"

12:5 Greek *300 denarii.* A denarius was equivalent to a full day's wage.   **12:9** Greek *Jewish people;* also in 12:11.   **12:13a** Greek *Hosanna,* an exclamation of praise that literally means "save now."   **12:13b** Ps 118:25–26; Zeph 3:15.   **12:15a** Greek *daughter of Zion.*   **12:15b** Zech 9:9.

²⁰Some Greeks who had come to Jerusalem to attend the Passover ²¹paid a visit to Philip, who was from Bethsaida in Galilee. They said, "Sir, we want to meet Jesus." ²²Philip told Andrew about it, and they went together to ask Jesus.

²³Jesus replied, "The time has come for the Son of Man to enter into his glory. ²⁴The truth is, a kernel of wheat must be planted in the soil. Unless it dies it will be alone—a single seed. But its death will produce many new kernels—a plentiful harvest of new lives. ²⁵Those who love their life in this world will lose it. Those who despise their life in this world will keep it for eternal life. ²⁶All those who want to be my disciples must come and follow me, because my servants must be where I am. And if they follow me, the Father will honor them. ²⁷Now my soul is deeply troubled. Should I pray, 'Father, save me from what lies ahead'? But that is the very reason why I came! ²⁸Father, bring glory to your name."

Then a voice spoke from heaven, saying, "I have already brought it glory, and I will do it again." ²⁹When the crowd heard the voice, some thought it was thunder, while others declared an angel had spoken to him.

³⁰Then Jesus told them, "The voice was for your benefit, not mine. ³¹The time of judgment for the world has come, when the prince of this world* will be cast out. ³²And when I am lifted up on the cross,* I will draw everyone to myself." ³³He said this to indicate how he was going to die.

³⁴"Die?" asked the crowd. "We understood from Scripture that the Messiah would live forever. Why are you saying the Son of Man will die? Who is this Son of Man you are talking about?"

³⁵Jesus replied, "My light will shine out for you just a little while longer. Walk in it while you can, so you will not stumble when the darkness falls. If you walk in the darkness, you cannot see where you are going. ³⁶Believe in the light while there is still time; then you will become children of the light." After saying these things, Jesus went away and was hidden from them.

³⁷But despite all the miraculous signs he had done, most of the

12:31 *The prince of this world* is a name for Satan. **12:32** Greek *lifted up from the earth.*

people did not believe in him. ³⁸This is exactly what Isaiah the prophet had predicted:

"Lord, who has believed our message?
   To whom will the Lord reveal his saving power?"*

³⁹But the people couldn't believe, for as Isaiah also said,

40 "The Lord has blinded their eyes
      and hardened their hearts—
   so their eyes cannot see,
      and their hearts cannot understand,
   and they cannot turn to me
      and let me heal them."*

⁴¹Isaiah was referring to Jesus when he made this prediction, because he was given a vision of the Messiah's glory. ⁴²Many people, including some of the Jewish leaders, believed in him. But they wouldn't admit it to anyone because of their fear that the Pharisees would expel them from the synagogue. ⁴³For they loved human praise more than the praise of God.

⁴⁴Jesus shouted to the crowds, "If you trust me, you are really trusting God who sent me. ⁴⁵For when you see me, you are seeing the one who sent me. ⁴⁶I have come as a light to shine in this dark world, so that all who put their trust in me will no longer remain in the darkness. ⁴⁷If anyone hears me and doesn't obey me, I am not his judge—for I have come to save the world and not to judge it. ⁴⁸But all who reject me and my message will be judged at the day of judgment by the truth I have spoken. ⁴⁹I don't speak on my own authority. The Father who sent me gave me his own instructions as to what I should say. ⁵⁰And I know his instructions lead to eternal life; so I say whatever the Father tells me to say!"

Reflect ...

In this chapter, it is very clear that the religious leaders (who would not accept Jesus as the Son of God) were plotting to kill Jesus and Lazarus.

12:38 Isa 53:1. **12:40** Isa 6:10.

Why Lazarus? Well, Lazarus represented one of the most incredible miracles that Jesus ever performed. Because of Lazarus, many people believed in Jesus. The religious leaders didn't believe. They only got angry and wanted to do away with the evidence.

Satan will do anything to weaken the argument that Jesus is truly the Savior of the world. He'll try to make you forget about the miracles that Jesus has performed in your life and in the lives of others. He'll try to get rid of all the evidence.

Respond ...

Try to remember some of the miracles that Jesus has performed in your life. Write them down. Include the circumstances surrounding them. How has God answered your prayers? How has Jesus given life to you?

_____

_____

_____

_____

_____

_____

When you pray, ask God to keep your memory fresh. Ask Him to prevent Satan from filling your head with doubts about who Jesus is and what He has done in your life.

• Chapter Thirteen •

"Follow the Leader"

Read . . .

Jesus never asks us to do anything that He wouldn't or didn't do himself. In this story, Jesus actually got down and dirty to bless His disciples. He does something that would be a challenge for all of us to do for someone else. As you read, ask yourself this question: Am I ready to love people the same way Jesus demonstrated His love?

John•Chapter 13

Before the Passover celebration, Jesus knew that his hour had come to leave this world and return to his Father. He now showed the disciples the full extent of his love.* ²It was time for supper, and the Devil had already enticed Judas, son of Simon Iscariot, to carry out his plan to betray Jesus. ³Jesus knew that the Father had given him authority over everything and that he had come from God and would return to God. ⁴So he got up from the table, took off his robe, wrapped a towel around his waist, ⁵and poured water into a basin. Then he began to wash the disciples' feet and to wipe them with the towel he had around him.

⁶When he came to Simon Peter, Peter said to him, "Lord, why are you going to wash my feet?"

13:1 Or *He loved his disciples to the very end.*

⁷Jesus replied, "You don't understand now why I am doing it; someday you will."

⁸"No," Peter protested, "you will never wash my feet!"

Jesus replied, "But if I don't wash you, you won't belong to me."

⁹Simon Peter exclaimed, "Then wash my hands and head as well, Lord, not just my feet!"

¹⁰Jesus replied, "A person who has bathed all over does not need to wash, except for the feet,* to be entirely clean. And you are clean, but that isn't true of everyone here." ¹¹For Jesus knew who would betray him. That is what he meant when he said, "Not all of you are clean."

¹²After washing their feet, he put on his robe again and sat down and asked, "Do you understand what I was doing? ¹³You call me 'Teacher' and 'Lord,' and you are right, because it is true. ¹⁴And since I, the Lord and Teacher, have washed your feet, you ought to wash each other's feet. ¹⁵I have given you an example to follow. Do as I have done to you. ¹⁶How true it is that a servant is not greater than the master. Nor are messengers more important than the one who sends them. ¹⁷You know these things—now do them! That is the path of blessing.

¹⁸"I am not saying these things to all of you; I know so well each one of you I chose. The Scriptures declare, 'The one who shares my food has turned against me,'* and this will soon come true. ¹⁹I tell you this now, so that when it happens you will believe I am the Messiah. ²⁰Truly, anyone who welcomes my messenger is welcoming me, and anyone who welcomes me is welcoming the Father who sent me."

²¹Now Jesus was in great anguish of spirit, and he exclaimed, "The truth is, one of you will betray me!"

²²The disciples looked at each other, wondering whom he could mean. ²³One of Jesus' disciples, the one Jesus loved, was sitting next to Jesus at the table.* ²⁴Simon Peter motioned to him to ask who would do this terrible thing. ²⁵Leaning toward Jesus, he asked, "Lord, who is it?"

13:10 Some manuscripts do not include *except for the feet.* 13:18 Ps 41:9. 13:23 Greek *was reclining on Jesus' bosom.* The "disciple whom Jesus loved" was probably John.

²⁶Jesus said, "It is the one to whom I give the bread dipped in the sauce." And when he had dipped it, he gave it to Judas, son of Simon Iscariot. ²⁷As soon as Judas had eaten the bread, Satan entered into him. Then Jesus told him, "Hurry. Do it now." ²⁸None of the others at the table knew what Jesus meant. ²⁹Since Judas was their treasurer, some thought Jesus was telling him to go and pay for the food or to give some money to the poor. ³⁰So Judas left at once, going out into the night.

³¹As soon as Judas left the room, Jesus said, "The time has come for me, the Son of Man, to enter into my glory, and God will receive glory because of all that happens to me. ³²And God will bring* me into my glory very soon. ³³Dear children, how brief are these moments before I must go away and leave you! Then, though you search for me, you cannot come to me—just as I told the Jewish leaders. ³⁴So now I am giving you a new commandment: Love each other. Just as I have loved you, you should love each other. ³⁵Your love for one another will prove to the world that you are my disciples."

³⁶Simon Peter said, "Lord, where are you going?"

And Jesus replied, "You can't go with me now, but you will follow me later."

³⁷"But why can't I come now, Lord?" he asked. "I am ready to die for you."

³⁸Jesus answered, "Die for me? No, before the rooster crows tomorrow morning, you will deny three times that you even know me.

Reflect ...

Jesus washed His disciples' feet as an act of humility and kindness. Because "a servant is not greater than the master," we are obligated, out of our love for God, to follow His example. What He does for others, we need to do for others.

This doesn't necessarily mean washing the feet of everyone you meet, but there are other ways to show humility and kind-

13:32 Some manuscripts read *And if God is glorified in him [the Son of Man], God will bring.*

ness. What things has Jesus done for you that you need to do for others? Acts of kindness? Forgiveness? Love?

Respond ...

Write the name of one person whom you will treat with humility and kindness, as Jesus would do. Also write down what you will do.

_____

_____

_____

_____

_____

_____

When you pray, ask God to help you become more humble and kind to others in obedience to the example of Jesus.

• Chapter Fourteen •

One Way!

Read ...

One of the things Christians believe is that Jesus is going to return someday. He will come to get all those who believe in Him and take them back to heaven. This is what the Bible teaches.

But it has been a long time since Jesus made the promise to return. This doesn't mean that He won't return; it only means that we are now closer to the time of the Lord's return than ever before. Still, it's easy to get discouraged and wonder if it's ever going to happen.

As you read today, focus on verses 1–7 and ask God to encourage your heart.

John●Chapter 14

"Don't be troubled. You trust God, now trust in me. ²There are many rooms in my Father's home, and I am going to prepare a place for you. If this were not so, I would tell you plainly. ³When everything is ready, I will come and get you, so that you will always be with me where I am. ⁴And you know where I am going and how to get there."

⁵"No, we don't know, Lord," Thomas said. "We haven't any idea where you are going, so how can we know the way?"

⁶Jesus told him, "I am the way, the truth, and the life. No one

can come to the Father except through me. [7]If you had known who I am, then you would have known who my Father is.* From now on you know him and have seen him!"

[8]Philip said, "Lord, show us the Father and we will be satisfied."

[9]Jesus replied, "Philip, don't you even yet know who I am, even after all the time I have been with you? Anyone who has seen me has seen the Father! So why are you asking to see him? [10]Don't you believe that I am in the Father and the Father is in me? The words I say are not my own, but my Father who lives in me does his work through me. [11]Just believe that I am in the Father and the Father is in me. Or at least believe because of what you have seen me do.

[12]"The truth is, anyone who believes in me will do the same works I have done, and even greater works, because I am going to be with the Father. [13]You can ask for anything in my name, and I will do it, because the work of the Son brings glory to the Father. [14]Yes, ask anything in my name, and I will do it!

[15]"If you love me, obey my commandments. [16]And I will ask the Father, and he will give you another Counselor,* who will never leave you. [17]He is the Holy Spirit, who leads into all truth. The world at large cannot receive him, because it isn't looking for him and doesn't recognize him. But you do, because he lives with you now and later will be in you. [18]No, I will not abandon you as orphans—I will come to you. [19]In just a little while the world will not see me again, but you will. For I will live again, and you will, too. [20]When I am raised to life again, you will know that I am in my Father, and you are in me, and I am in you. [21]Those who obey my commandments are the ones who love me. And because they love me, my Father will love them, and I will love them. And I will reveal myself to each one of them."

[22]Judas (not Judas Iscariot, but the other disciple with that name) said to him, "Lord, why are you going to reveal yourself only to us and not to the world at large?"

[23]Jesus replied, "All those who love me will do what I say. My

14:7 Some manuscripts read *If you really have known me, you will know who my Father is.* **14:16** Or *Comforter,* or *Encourager,* or *Advocate.* Greek *Paraclete;* also in 14:26.

Father will love them, and we will come to them and live with them. ²⁴Anyone who doesn't love me will not do what I say. And remember, my words are not my own. This message is from the Father who sent me. ²⁵I am telling you these things now while I am still with you. ²⁶But when the Father sends the Counselor as my representative—and by the Counselor I mean the Holy Spirit—he will teach you everything and will remind you of everything I myself have told you.

²⁷"I am leaving you with a gift—peace of mind and heart. And the peace I give isn't like the peace the world gives. So don't be troubled or afraid. ²⁸Remember what I told you: I am going away, but I will come back to you again. If you really love me, you will be very happy for me, because now I can go to the Father, who is greater than I am. ²⁹I have told you these things before they happen so that you will believe when they do happen.

³⁰"I don't have much more time to talk to you, because the prince of this world approaches. He has no power over me, ³¹but I will do what the Father requires of me, so that the world will know that I love the Father. Come, let's be going."

Reflect ...

Jesus made it very clear. He is coming back to get us. Not only is He coming back, but He is preparing a place for us right now—a mansion in heaven!

Would you like to live eternally in a beautiful mansion? It sure beats the alternatives, doesn't it? How can you be sure that you will go to heaven? Jesus gave us the answer: *"I am the way, the truth, and the life. No one can come to the Father except through me"* (John 14:6). Jesus didn't say this to keep anybody out of heaven; He said it to tell people how to get into heaven.

Jesus wants us to trust Him completely as the way to have happiness and security. Nothing else will do.

Respond ...

Do you trust Christ completely? List some of the other things you sometimes trust in to give you happiness and security.

_____

_____

_____

_____

_____

_____

When you pray, ask God to give you more faith so you won't trust in the "other things" for the happiness and security that only Christ can deliver.

Congratulations! You are two-thirds of the way through your 21 Jump-Start Program.

• Chapter Fifteen •

The Main Thing

Read ...

It may seem to you that there are a lot of rules and commandments to learn when you become a Christian. Yes, it's true. There is a lot of stuff to learn, and it can take a lifetime to make all you learn part of your everyday routine.

That's why on several occasions Jesus tried to summarize the BIG IDEA behind all the rules and commandments. He doesn't want us to get bogged down in hundreds of rules. He wants us to remember that the "main thing" is to "make the main thing the main thing." What is the "main thing"? Focus your reading on verses 1–17.

John•Chapter 15

"I am the true vine, and my Father is the gardener. ²He cuts off every branch that doesn't produce fruit, and he prunes the branches that do bear fruit so they will produce even more. ³You have already been pruned for greater fruitfulness by the message I have given you. ⁴Remain in me, and I will remain in you. For a branch cannot produce fruit if it is severed from the vine, and you cannot be fruitful apart from me.

⁵"Yes, I am the vine; you are the branches. Those who remain in me, and I in them, will produce much fruit. For apart from me you can do nothing. ⁶Anyone who parts from me is thrown away

like a useless branch and withers. Such branches are gathered into a pile to be burned. [7]But if you stay joined to me and my words remain in you, you may ask any request you like, and it will be granted! [8]My true disciples produce much fruit. This brings great glory to my Father.

[9]"I have loved you even as the Father has loved me. Remain in my love. [10]When you obey me, you remain in my love, just as I obey my Father and remain in his love. [11]I have told you this so that you will be filled with my joy. Yes, your joy will overflow! [12]I command you to love each other in the same way that I love you. [13]And here is how to measure it—the greatest love is shown when people lay down their lives for their friends. [14]You are my friends if you obey me. [15]I no longer call you servants, because a master doesn't confide in his servants. Now you are my friends, since I have told you everything the Father told me. [16]You didn't choose me. I chose you. I appointed you to go and produce fruit that will last, so that the Father will give you whatever you ask for, using my name. [17]I command you to love each other.

[18]"When the world hates you, remember it hated me before it hated you. [19]The world would love you if you belonged to it, but you don't. I chose you to come out of the world, and so it hates you. [20]Do you remember what I told you? 'A servant is not greater than the master.' Since they persecuted me, naturally they will persecute you. And if they had listened to me, they would listen to you! [21]The people of the world will hate you because you belong to me, for they don't know God who sent me. [22]They would not be guilty if I had not come and spoken to them. But now they have no excuse for their sin. [23]Anyone who hates me hates my Father, too. [24]If I hadn't done such miraculous signs among them that no one else could do, they would not be counted guilty. But as it is, they saw all that I did and yet hated both of us—me and my Father. [25]This has fulfilled what the Scriptures said: 'They hated me without cause.'*

[26]"But I will send you the Counselor*—the Spirit of truth. He will come to you from the Father and will tell you all about me.

15:25 Pss 35:19; 69:4. **15:26** Or *Comforter*, or *Encourager*, or *Advocate*. Greek *Paraclete*.

[27]And you must also tell others about me because you have been with me from the beginning."

Reflect ...

Just as a TV set must be plugged into the wall to get the electricity it needs, we have to stay plugged into Jesus in order to have the power we need to serve and obey Him.

Jesus commands us to love each other just as He loves us. Can you do it? Probably not—unless you are plugged into Jesus. You must continually trust Him by faith to help you "make the main thing the main thing."

Respond ...

In the space below, write down three ways you could show love to someone else today.

_____

_____

_____

_____

_____

When you pray, commit yourself to be a more loving person.

• Chapter Sixteen •

Promise Keeper

Read ...

Jesus never made following Him sound easy. He made it very clear that it would be hard and that people would persecute those who followed Him.

But in this chapter, Jesus offers encouragement and comfort to all His disciples by promising to send help in time of need. See if you can identify this promise and determine how it has already been fulfilled in your life.

John•Chapter 16

"I have told you these things so that you won't fall away. ²For you will be expelled from the synagogues, and the time is coming when those who kill you will think they are doing God a service. ³This is because they have never known the Father or me. ⁴Yes, I'm telling you these things now, so that when they happen, you will remember I warned you. I didn't tell you earlier because I was going to be with you for a while longer.

⁵"But now I am going away to the one who sent me, and none of you has asked me where I am going. ⁶Instead, you are very sad. ⁷But it is actually best for you that I go away, because if I don't, the Counselor* won't come. If I do go away, he will come because I will send him to you. ⁸And when he comes, he will convince

16:7 Or *Comforter*, or *Encourager*, or *Advocate*. Greek *Paraclete*.

the world of its sin, and of God's righteousness, and of the coming judgment. [9]The world's sin is unbelief in me. [10]Righteousness is available because I go to the Father, and you will see me no more. [11]Judgment will come because the prince of this world has already been judged.

[12]"Oh, there is so much more I want to tell you, but you can't bear it now. [13]When the Spirit of truth comes, he will guide you into all truth. He will not be presenting his own ideas; he will be telling you what he has heard. He will tell you about the future. [14]He will bring me glory by revealing to you whatever he receives from me. [15]All that the Father has is mine; this is what I mean when I say that the Spirit will reveal to you whatever he receives from me.

[16]"In just a little while I will be gone, and you won't see me anymore. Then, just a little while after that, you will see me again."

[17]The disciples asked each other, "What does he mean when he says, 'You won't see me, and then you will see me'? And what does he mean when he says, 'I am going to the Father'? [18]And what does he mean by 'a little while'? We don't understand."

[19]Jesus realized they wanted to ask him, so he said, "Are you asking yourselves what I meant? I said in just a little while I will be gone, and you won't see me anymore. Then, just a little while after that, you will see me again. [20]Truly, you will weep and mourn over what is going to happen to me, but the world will rejoice. You will grieve, but your grief will suddenly turn to wonderful joy when you see me again. [21]It will be like a woman experiencing the pains of labor. When her child is born, her anguish gives place to joy because she has brought a new person into the world. [22]You have sorrow now, but I will see you again; then you will rejoice, and no one can rob you of that joy. [23]At that time you won't need to ask me for anything. The truth is, you can go directly to the Father and ask him, and he will grant your request because you use my name. [24]You haven't done this before. Ask, using my name, and you will receive, and you will have abundant joy.

[25]"I have spoken of these matters in parables, but the time will

come when this will not be necessary, and I will tell you plainly all about the Father. 26Then you will ask in my name. I'm not saying I will ask the Father on your behalf, 27for the Father himself loves you dearly because you love me and believe that I came from God. 28Yes, I came from the Father into the world, and I will leave the world and return to the Father."

29Then his disciples said, "At last you are speaking plainly and not in parables. 30Now we understand that you know everything and don't need anyone to tell you anything.* From this we believe that you came from God."

31Jesus asked, "Do you finally believe? 32But the time is coming—in fact, it is already here—when you will be scattered, each one going his own way, leaving me alone. Yet I am not alone because the Father is with me. 33I have told you all this so that you may have peace in me. Here on earth you will have many trials and sorrows. But take heart, because I have overcome the world."

Reflect ...

Jesus promised to send help. The name of that help is the Holy Spirit. After Jesus rose into heaven (see Acts 1), the Holy Spirit came in a special way (see Acts 2). Jesus also calls the Holy Spirit the "Spirit of Truth" and the "Counselor."

The role of the Holy Spirit is to dwell in our hearts, to lead and guide us through life. The Holy Spirit helps us understand that we are sinners in need of a Savior. The Holy Spirit also comforts us, encourages us, gives us insight into the Scriptures, and empowers us to do amazing things.

The Holy Spirit is God, just as Jesus is God and the Father is God. They are "three in one," or what we call "The Holy Trinity." You can talk to the Holy Spirit just as you talk to God and to Jesus in prayer.

16:30 Or *don't need that anyone should ask you anything.*

Respond ...

In the space below, write down some specific areas of your life where you need more encouragement, more wisdom, or more power. Try to be specific.

_____

_____

_____

_____

_____

_____

When you pray, ask the Holy Spirit to give you the encouragement, wisdom, and power you need.

• Chapter Seventeen •

Pray for Me!

Read ...

When you give your life to Jesus, you are sent out to live for Him in the world. Do you have to live the Christian life on your own? No way! As you read this chapter, you will see that Jesus is praying for you right now. What is His prayer for you?

John•Chapter 17

When Jesus had finished saying all these things, he looked up to heaven and said, "Father, the time has come. Glorify your Son so he can give glory back to you. ²For you have given him authority over everyone in all the earth. He gives eternal life to each one you have given him. ³And this is the way to have eternal life—to know you, the only true God, and Jesus Christ, the one you sent to earth. ⁴I brought glory to you here on earth by doing everything you told me to do. ⁵And now, Father, bring me into the glory we shared before the world began.

⁶"I have told these men about you. They were in the world, but then you gave them to me. Actually, they were always yours, and you gave them to me; and they have kept your word. ⁷Now they know that everything I have is a gift from you, ⁸for I have passed on to them the words you gave me; and they accepted them and know that I came from you, and they believe you sent me.

⁹"My prayer is not for the world, but for those you have given me, because they belong to you. ¹⁰And all of them, since they are mine, belong to you; and you have given them back to me, so they are my glory! ¹¹Now I am departing the world; I am leaving them behind and coming to you. Holy Father, keep them and care for them—all those you have given me—so that they will be united just as we are. ¹²During my time here, I have kept them safe.* I guarded them so that not one was lost, except the one headed for destruction, as the Scriptures foretold.

¹³"And now I am coming to you. I have told them many things while I was with them so they would be filled with my joy. ¹⁴I have given them your word. And the world hates them because they do not belong to the world, just as I do not. ¹⁵I'm not asking you to take them out of the world, but to keep them safe from the evil one. ¹⁶They are not part of this world any more than I am. ¹⁷Make them pure and holy by teaching them your words of truth. ¹⁸As you sent me into the world, I am sending them into the world. ¹⁹And I give myself entirely to you so they also might be entirely yours.

²⁰"I am praying not only for these disciples but also for all who will ever believe in me because of their testimony. ²¹My prayer for all of them is that they will be one, just as you and I are one, Father—that just as you are in me and I am in you, so they will be in us, and the world will believe you sent me.

²²"I have given them the glory you gave me, so that they may be one, as we are—²³I in them and you in me, all being perfected into one. Then the world will know that you sent me and will understand that you love them as much as you love me. ²⁴Father, I want these whom you've given me to be with me, so they can see my glory. You gave me the glory because you loved me even before the world began!

²⁵"O righteous Father, the world doesn't know you, but I do; and these disciples know you sent me. ²⁶And I have revealed you to them and will keep on revealing you. I will do this so that your love for me may be in them and I in them."

17:12 Greek *I have kept in your name those whom you have given me.*

Reflect ...

This chapter contains what is often called "Christ's Prayer for the Church." It gives us great insight into the heart of our Lord and the prayer He prayed on our behalf. Jesus was getting ready to die on the cross, but He still found time to pray for His disciples and to pray for all those who would believe in Him in the future.

Hey, that's you! In this prayer, Jesus prays *for you and me and all of us* who have been called out of the world to follow Him. As you can tell from this prayer, Jesus loves you and desires great things for you.

Jesus continues to pray for you today. He takes your cares and needs to the Father. What do you want Jesus to pray for you today?

Respond ...

In Jesus' prayer, He prayed that we would all be one—that we would love one another and be united in spirit and truth. In what other ways would you want Jesus to pray for you today?

_____

_____

_____

_____

_____

_____

When you pray, take your needs and cares to Jesus. He will take them to the Father.

Chapter Eighteen

Time for a Drink?

Read ...

In the next two chapters, you will read about Jesus being betrayed by a friend, lied about, and falsely accused by religious leaders. When He is first betrayed by Judas, the soldiers come to get Him as though He were a common criminal. Some of the disciples want to fight back to protect Jesus. As you read closely, note that Jesus does not fight back. He instead accepts what is being done to Him and goes quietly. We find the key to His calm attitude in the first eleven verses of this chapter. What is it?

John•Chapter 18

After saying these things, Jesus crossed the Kidron Valley with his disciples and entered a grove of olive trees. ²Judas, the betrayer, knew this place, because Jesus had gone there many times with his disciples. ³The leading priests and Pharisees had given Judas a battalion of Roman soldiers and Temple guards to accompany him. Now with blazing torches, lanterns, and weapons, they arrived at the olive grove.

⁴Jesus fully realized all that was going to happen to him. Stepping forward to meet them, he asked, "Whom are you looking for?"

⁵"Jesus of Nazareth," they replied.

"I am he,"* Jesus said. Judas was standing there with them when Jesus identified himself. ⁶And as he said, "I am he," they all fell backward to the ground! ⁷Once more he asked them, "Whom are you searching for?"

And again they replied, "Jesus of Nazareth."

⁸"I told you that I am he," Jesus said. "And since I am the one you want, let these others go." ⁹He did this to fulfill his own statement: "I have not lost a single one of those you gave me."*

¹⁰Then Simon Peter drew a sword and slashed off the right ear of Malchus, the high priest's servant. ¹¹But Jesus said to Peter, "Put your sword back into its sheath. Shall I not drink from the cup the Father has given me?"

¹²So the soldiers, their commanding officer, and the Temple guards arrested Jesus and tied him up. ¹³First they took him to Annas, the father-in-law of Caiaphas, the high priest that year. ¹⁴Caiaphas was the one who had told the other Jewish leaders, "Better that one should die for all."

¹⁵Simon Peter followed along behind, as did another of the disciples. That other disciple was acquainted with the high priest, so he was allowed to enter the courtyard with Jesus. ¹⁶Peter stood outside the gate. Then the other disciple spoke to the woman watching at the gate, and she let Peter in. ¹⁷The woman asked Peter, "Aren't you one of Jesus' disciples?"

"No," he said, "I am not."

¹⁸The guards and the household servants were standing around a charcoal fire they had made because it was cold. And Peter stood there with them, warming himself.

¹⁹Inside, the high priest began asking Jesus about his followers and what he had been teaching them. ²⁰Jesus replied, "What I teach is widely known, because I have preached regularly in the synagogues and the Temple. I have been heard by people* everywhere, and I teach nothing in private that I have not said in public. ²¹Why are you asking me this question? Ask those who heard me. They know what I said."

²²One of the Temple guards standing there struck Jesus on the face. "Is that the way to answer the high priest?" he demanded.

18:5 Greek *I am;* also in 18:6, 8.   18:9 See John 6:39 and 17:12.   18:20 Greek *Jewish people;* also in 18:38.

²³Jesus replied, "If I said anything wrong, you must give evidence for it. Should you hit a man for telling the truth?"

²⁴Then Annas bound Jesus and sent him to Caiaphas, the high priest.

²⁵Meanwhile, as Simon Peter was standing by the fire, they asked him again, "Aren't you one of his disciples?"

"I am not," he said.

²⁶But one of the household servants of the high priest, a relative of the man whose ear Peter had cut off, asked, "Didn't I see you out there in the olive grove with Jesus?" ²⁷Again Peter denied it. And immediately a rooster crowed.

²⁸Jesus' trial before Caiaphas ended in the early hours of the morning. Then he was taken to the headquarters of the Roman governor. His accusers didn't go in themselves because it would defile them, and they wouldn't be allowed to celebrate the Passover feast. ²⁹So Pilate, the governor, went out to them and asked, "What is your charge against this man?"

³⁰"We wouldn't have handed him over to you if he weren't a criminal!" they retorted.

³¹"Then take him away and judge him by your own laws," Pilate told them.

"Only the Romans are permitted to execute someone," the Jewish leaders replied. ³²This fulfilled Jesus' prediction about the way he would die.*

³³Then Pilate went back inside and called for Jesus to be brought to him. "Are you the King of the Jews?" he asked him.

³⁴Jesus replied, "Is this your own question, or did others tell you about me?"

³⁵"Am I a Jew?" Pilate asked. "Your own people and their leading priests brought you here. Why? What have you done?"

³⁶Then Jesus answered, "I am not an earthly king. If I were, my followers would have fought when I was arrested by the Jewish leaders. But my Kingdom is not of this world."

³⁷Pilate replied, "You are a king then?"

"You say that I am a king, and you are right," Jesus said. "I was born for that purpose. And I came to bring truth to the world.

18:32 See John 12:32–33.

All who love the truth recognize that what I say is true.''

[38]"What is truth?'' Pilate asked. Then he went out again to the people and told them, "He is not guilty of any crime. [39]But you have a custom of asking me to release someone from prison each year at Passover. So if you want me to, I'll release the King of the Jews.''

[40]But they shouted back, "No! Not this man, but Barabbas!'' (Barabbas was a criminal.)

Reflect ...

In verse 11, Jesus tells His disciples not to fight the soldiers because He is ready and willing to "drink the cup'' that was given to Him by his Father. What did He mean?

Essentially, Jesus meant that He was committed to obeying God—no matter what. This verse helps us to understand how Jesus could have such a calm attitude in the middle of a dangerous situation. Regardless of the circumstances, Jesus was completely focused on doing God's will. He was ready to "drink the cup'' which His Father had offered to Him, even if it meant He would suffer.

God also has a cup for you to drink. What do you think it is? Is there something God wants you to do today that does not seem like it will be fun or easy?

Respond ...

In the space below, try to describe the "cup'' that God has given you to drink. What do you think He wants you to do with it?

_____

_____

_____

_____

_____

_____

When you pray, ask God to give you the courage to drink the cup He has given to you.

• Chapter Nineteen •

Getting Focused

Read ...

As you read this chapter, make a note of all the cruel things that were done to Jesus. Be sure to include anything that would add to His physical, mental, and emotional suffering. Then get prepared to be challenged.

John•Chapter 19

Then Pilate had Jesus flogged with a lead-tipped whip. ²The soldiers made a crown of long, sharp thorns and put it on his head, and they put a royal purple robe on him. ³"Hail! King of the Jews!" they mocked, and they hit him with their fists.

⁴Pilate went outside again and said to the people, "I am going to bring him out to you now, but understand clearly that I find him not guilty." ⁵Then Jesus came out wearing the crown of thorns and the purple robe. And Pilate said, "Here is the man!"

⁶When they saw him, the leading priests and Temple guards began shouting, "Crucify! Crucify!"

"You crucify him," Pilate said. "I find him not guilty."

⁷The Jewish leaders replied, "By our laws he ought to die because he called himself the Son of God."

⁸When Pilate heard this, he was more frightened than ever. ⁹He took Jesus back into the headquarters again and asked him, "Where are you from?" But Jesus gave no answer. ¹⁰"You won't

talk to me?" Pilate demanded. "Don't you realize that I have the power to release you or to crucify you?"

¹¹Then Jesus said, "You would have no power over me at all unless it were given to you from above. So the one who brought me to you has the greater sin."

¹²Then Pilate tried to release him, but the Jewish leaders told him, "If you release this man, you are not a friend of Caesar. Anyone who declares himself a king is a rebel against Caesar."

¹³When they said this, Pilate brought Jesus out to them again. Then Pilate sat down on the judgment seat on the platform that is called the Stone Pavement (in Hebrew, *Gabbatha*). ¹⁴It was now about noon of the day of preparation for the Passover. And Pilate said to the people,* "Here is your king!"

¹⁵"Away with him," they yelled. "Away with him—crucify him!"

"What? Crucify your king?" Pilate asked.

"We have no king but Caesar," the leading priests shouted back.

¹⁶Then Pilate gave Jesus to them to be crucified.

So they took Jesus and led him away. ¹⁷Carrying the cross by himself, Jesus went to the place called Skull Hill (in Hebrew, *Golgotha*). ¹⁸There they crucified him. There were two others crucified with him, one on either side, with Jesus between them. ¹⁹And Pilate posted a sign over him that read, "Jesus of Nazareth, the King of the Jews." ²⁰The place where Jesus was crucified was near the city; and the sign was written in Hebrew, Latin, and Greek, so that many people could read it.

²¹Then the leading priests said to Pilate, "Change it from 'The King of the Jews' to 'He said, I am King of the Jews.' "

²²Pilate replied, "What I have written, I have written. It stays exactly as it is."

²³When the soldiers had crucified Jesus, they divided his clothes among the four of them. They also took his robe, but it was seamless, woven in one piece from the top. ²⁴So they said, "Let's not tear it but throw dice* to see who gets it." This fulfilled the Scripture that says, "They divided my clothes among them-

19:14 Greek *Jewish people;* also in 19:20.   19:24a Greek *cast lots.*

selves and threw dice for my robe."* So that is what they did.

²⁵Standing near the cross were Jesus' mother, and his mother's sister, Mary (the wife of Clopas), and Mary Magdalene. ²⁶When Jesus saw his mother standing there beside the disciple he loved, he said to her, "Woman, he is your son." ²⁷And he said to this disciple, "She is your mother." And from then on this disciple took her into his home.

²⁸Jesus knew that everything was now finished, and to fulfill the Scriptures he said, "I am thirsty."* ²⁹A jar of sour wine was sitting there, so they soaked a sponge in it, put it on a hyssop branch, and held it up to his lips. ³⁰When Jesus had tasted it, he said, "It is finished!" Then he bowed his head and gave up his spirit.

³¹The Jewish leaders didn't want the victims hanging there the next day, which was the Sabbath (and a very special Sabbath at that, because it was the Passover), so they asked Pilate to hasten their deaths by ordering that their legs be broken. Then their bodies could be taken down. ³²So the soldiers came and broke the legs of the two men crucified with Jesus. ³³But when they came to Jesus, they saw that he was dead already, so they didn't break his legs. ³⁴One of the soldiers, however, pierced his side with a spear, and blood and water flowed out. ³⁵This report is from an eyewitness giving an accurate account; it is presented so that you also can believe. ³⁶These things happened in fulfillment of the Scriptures that say, "Not one of his bones will be broken,"* ³⁷and "They will look on him whom they pierced."*

³⁸Afterward Joseph of Arimathea, who had been a secret disciple of Jesus (because he feared the Jewish leaders), asked Pilate for permission to take Jesus' body down. When Pilate gave him permission, he came and took the body away. ³⁹Nicodemus, the man who had come to Jesus at night, also came, bringing about seventy-five pounds* of embalming ointment made from myrrh and aloes. ⁴⁰Together they wrapped Jesus' body in a long linen cloth with the spices, as is the Jewish custom of burial. ⁴¹The place of crucifixion was near a garden, where there was a new

19:24b Ps 22:18.   **19:28** See Pss 22:15; 69:21.   **19:36** Exod 12:46; Num 9:12; Ps 34:20.   **19:37** Zech 12:10.   **19:39** Greek *100 litras* [32.7 kilograms].

tomb, never used before. [42]And so, because it was the day of preparation before the Passover and since the tomb was close at hand, they laid Jesus there.

Reflect ...

In verse 30, Jesus says, "It is finished." What do you think He was talking about? The world was still a mess. His disciples were running scared. His mother was crying. The devil thought He had killed God.

Jesus had a specific responsibility. He came to die for our sins. Despite the suffering He had to endure, He did it willingly. He did not come into the world to fix everyone's problems, heal all the sick, or to make everyone a Christian before He left. He came to die and He finished the job on the cross.

But He did leave us here to continue doing what He did while He was on earth. He told His disciples to go and make disciples (Matthew 28:19) and He gave us the Holy Spirit, who has given us all spiritual gifts (abilities) to use for the benefit of others (see 1 Corinthians 12).

Respond ...

What abilities has God given you that could be used for the benefit of others? How do you plan to use them? What kind of ministry would you like to get involved in? Will you?

_____

_____

_____

_____

_____

When you pray, ask God to help you finish the work and ministry that He has called you to do.

• Chapter Twenty •

Seeing Is Believing

Read ...

Because it requires faith to follow Jesus, there are aspects of Christianity that don't make sense to our natural way of thinking. All the miracles that Jesus performed were supernatural, which is why many people don't believe they really happened. It requires faith to believe that the Word of God is true.

In this chapter, you will read about Thomas, one of Jesus' disciples, who had a hard time believing that Jesus really rose from the dead. Jesus' resurrection was more than Thomas's natural mind could handle.

When the risen Jesus finally caught up with Thomas, what do you think Thomas said?

John•Chapter 20

Early Sunday morning,* while it was still dark, Mary Magdalene came to the tomb and found that the stone had been rolled away from the entrance. ²She ran and found Simon Peter and the other disciple, the one whom Jesus loved. She said, "They have taken the Lord's body out of the tomb, and I don't know where they have put him!"

20:1 Greek *On the first day of the week.*

³Peter and the other disciple ran to the tomb to see. ⁴The other disciple outran Peter and got there first. ⁵He stooped and looked in and saw the linen cloth lying there, but he didn't go in. ⁶Then Simon Peter arrived and went inside. He also noticed the linen wrappings lying there, ⁷while the cloth that had covered Jesus' head was folded up and lying to the side. ⁸Then the other disciple also went in, and he saw and believed—⁹for until then they hadn't realized that the Scriptures said he would rise from the dead. ¹⁰Then they went home.

¹¹Mary was standing outside the tomb crying, and as she wept, she stooped and looked in. ¹²She saw two white-robed angels sitting at the head and foot of the place where the body of Jesus had been lying. ¹³"Why are you crying?" the angels asked her.

"Because they have taken away my Lord," she replied, "and I don't know where they have put him."

¹⁴She glanced over her shoulder and saw someone standing behind her. It was Jesus, but she didn't recognize him. ¹⁵"Why are you crying?" Jesus asked her. "Who are you looking for?"

She thought he was the gardener. "Sir," she said, "if you have taken him away, tell me where you have put him, and I will go and get him."

¹⁶"Mary!" Jesus said.

She turned toward him and exclaimed, "Teacher!"*

¹⁷"Don't cling to me," Jesus said, "for I haven't yet ascended to the Father. But go find my brothers and tell them that I am ascending to my Father and your Father, my God and your God."

¹⁸Mary Magdalene found the disciples and told them, "I have seen the Lord!" Then she gave them his message.

¹⁹That evening, on the first day of the week, the disciples were meeting behind locked doors because they were afraid of the Jewish leaders. Suddenly, Jesus was standing there among them! "Peace be with you," he said. ²⁰As he spoke, he held out his hands for them to see, and he showed them his side. They were filled with joy when they saw their Lord! ²¹He spoke to them again and said, "Peace be with you. As the Father has sent me, so I send you." ²²Then he breathed on them and said to them, "Receive the

20:16 Greek *and said in Hebrew, "Rabboni," which means "Teacher."*

Holy Spirit. [23]If you forgive anyone's sins, they are forgiven. If you refuse to forgive them, they are unforgiven."

[24]One of the disciples, Thomas (nicknamed the Twin*), was not with the others when Jesus came. [25]They told him, "We have seen the Lord!" But he replied, "I won't believe it unless I see the nail wounds in his hands, put my fingers into them, and place my hand into the wound in his side."

[26]Eight days later the disciples were together again, and this time Thomas was with them. The doors were locked; but suddenly, as before, Jesus was standing among them. He said, "Peace be with you." [27]Then he said to Thomas, "Put your finger here and see my hands. Put your hand into the wound in my side. Don't be faithless any longer. Believe!"

[28]"My Lord and my God!" Thomas exclaimed.

[29]Then Jesus told him, "You believe because you have seen me. Blessed are those who haven't seen me and believe anyway."

[30]Jesus' disciples saw him do many other miraculous signs besides the ones recorded in this book. [31]But these are written so that you may believe* that Jesus is the Messiah, the Son of God, and that by believing in him you will have life.

Reflect ...

When Thomas doubted the Resurrection, Jesus didn't scold him but gave him the evidence he needed. He told Thomas to look and touch. Immediately, "Doubting Thomas" became "Believing Thomas." Jesus said to him, in effect, "That's great, Thomas, but it's even better to have faith when you can't see or touch."

What proof do you need to believe in Jesus? Did He give it to you? Remember true faith believes even when there's no proof other than the Word of God.

20:24 Greek the one who was called Didymus. 20:31 Some manuscripts read may continue to believe.

Respond ...

Do you sometimes have doubts about the truth of the Gospel of Christ? Write down some of your doubts and what you would need to make those doubts go away.

_____

_____

_____

_____

_____

_____

When you pray, ask the Holy Spirit to fill your heart with assurance and to remove the doubts you have. Also ask Him to lead you to some mature Christians who can help you find the answers to the questions you have.

• Chapter Twenty-One •

What a Friend!

Read ...

As a kid, I went to church religiously every Sunday. I knew God was there in the church and I felt close to Him there, but I never realized that God also wanted to be close to me on Wednesday ... and Friday ... and Saturday night!

In this chapter, Jesus appears to His disciples for the third time since His resurrection from the dead. Notice how this encounter shows a side of Jesus you may have never noticed before: Jesus the good friend.

John•Chapter 21

Later Jesus appeared again to the disciples beside the Sea of Galilee.* This is how it happened. ²Several of the disciples were there—Simon Peter, Thomas (nicknamed the Twin*), Nathanael from Cana in Galilee, the sons of Zebedee, and two other disciples.

³Simon Peter said, "I'm going fishing."

"We'll come, too," they all said. So they went out in the boat, but they caught nothing all night.

⁴At dawn the disciples saw Jesus standing on the beach, but they couldn't see who he was. ⁵He called out, "Friends, have you caught any fish?"

21:1 Greek *Sea of Tiberias,* another name for the Sea of Galilee. **21:2** Greek *the one who was called Didymus.*

"No," they replied.

⁶Then he said, "Throw out your net on the right-hand side of the boat, and you'll get plenty of fish!" So they did, and they couldn't draw in the net because there were so many fish in it.

⁷Then the disciple whom Jesus loved said to Peter, "It is the Lord!" When Simon Peter heard that it was the Lord, he put on his tunic (for he had stripped for work), jumped into the water, and swam ashore. ⁸The others stayed with the boat and pulled the loaded net to the shore, for they were only out about three hundred feet.* ⁹When they got there, they saw that a charcoal fire was burning and fish were frying over it, and there was bread.

¹⁰"Bring some of the fish you've just caught," Jesus said. ¹¹So Simon Peter went aboard and dragged the net to the shore. There were 153 large fish, and yet the net hadn't torn.

¹²"Now come and have some breakfast!" Jesus said. And no one dared ask him if he really was the Lord because they were sure of it. ¹³Then Jesus served them the bread and the fish. ¹⁴This was the third time Jesus had appeared to his disciples since he had been raised from the dead.

¹⁵After breakfast Jesus said to Simon Peter, "Simon son of John, do you love me more than these?"

"Yes, Lord," Peter replied, "you know I love you."

"Then feed my lambs," Jesus told him.

¹⁶Jesus repeated the question: "Simon son of John, do you love me?"

"Yes, Lord," Peter said, "you know I love you."

"Then take care of my sheep," Jesus said.

¹⁷Once more he asked him, "Simon son of John, do you love me?"

Peter was grieved that Jesus asked the question a third time. He said, "Lord, you know everything. You know I love you."

Jesus said, "Then feed my sheep. ¹⁸The truth is, when you were young, you were able to do as you liked and go wherever you wanted to. But when you are old, you will stretch out your hands, and others will direct you and take you where you don't want to go." ¹⁹Jesus said this to let him know what kind of death

21:8 Greek *200 cubits* [90 meters].

he would die to glorify God. Then Jesus told him, "Follow me."

[20]Peter turned around and saw the disciple Jesus loved following them—the one who had leaned over to Jesus during supper and asked, "Lord, who among us will betray you?" [21]Peter asked Jesus, "What about him, Lord?"

[22]Jesus replied, "If I want him to remain alive until I return, what is that to you? You follow me." [23]So the rumor spread among the community of believers* that that disciple wouldn't die. But that isn't what Jesus said at all. He only said, "If I want him to remain alive until I return, what is that to you?"

[24]This is that disciple who saw these events and recorded them here. And we all know that his account of these things is accurate.

[25]And I suppose that if all the other things Jesus did were written down, the whole world could not contain the books.

Reflect ...

Many people will miss the blessing of God in their lives because they only look for God in the Church or in times of trouble, but that's not what the Bible teaches. Jesus is your friend. He wants to hang with you every day of the week, every month of the year, for the rest of your life.

God is present in your life every day and in all places. He is interested in you constantly. Look for Him and you will notice how He takes care of you. Give Him credit and honor for feeding you today, for putting clothes on your back, for giving you friends in your life, and for a roof over your head.

Throughout the day, stay aware of the blessings you receive from Him and those you would normally take for granted.

Respond ...

In the space below, write down some of the ways God has blessed you today, this week, and this month:

21:23 Greek the brothers.

_____

_____

_____

_____

_____

When you pray, thank God for His love and care for you. Thank Him for sending His Son to be your Savior and friend. Ask Him to make you more aware of His presence in your life.

Now What?

Congratulations! You have completed the 21 Jump-Start Program.

We hope and pray that you have established a habit of seeking God daily as you completed this book. But don't stop here. Continue to build on this good habit. You now understand how easy it is to read, reflect, and then respond on what you read in the Bible.

In other words, it should be pretty simple for you to continue to do your devotions every day. You could choose another book in the Bible to read and follow the same read, reflect and respond format. Try another one of the Gospels or the Psalms. Or you could go to your local Christian bookstore and buy another devotional for yourself.

You might be asking yourself, *Now what?* Well, I already thought of that for you. At the beginning of this book I listed ten "Say Whats" for you outlining your salvation. Now as you prepare for the rest of your Christian life, here are ten "Now Whats" for you to consider.

1. Join a church and get involved in a youth group.

Of the many things that come with salvation, one of them is a new family—a spiritual family. It will be in the church where you meet your spiritual family, people who believe in what you believe, and who are learning what you are learning. It will be in church where you sing, read, study the Bible together, as well as pray together. You will also share your burdens with one another, and your church family will help you grow as a Christian. Whatever church and youth group you attend, make sure that they teach you the Bible. Don't waste your time somewhere where all they do is play games. Only God's Word will change your life.

Read: Hebrews 10:24–25

2. Be baptized.

The Bible tells us to do many things once we have Jesus as Savior. One of the most important things to do is to be baptized. Once you have found a church, ask the pastor when you can be baptized. Just as Jesus went into the grave a dead man and rose from the dead with newness of life, going under the water represents your death to your sinful nature and coming up represents your rising with a new life.

Read: Acts 2:40–41

3. Share your faith.

Take a minute and think back to what you were like before you accepted Jesus as your Lord and Savior. Do you remember how lost and empty you felt? Many of your friends, classmates, and neighbors are like that now. The Bible says in Luke 12:48, *"But people who are not aware that they are doing wrong will be punished only lightly. Much is required from those to whom much is given, and much more is required from those to whom much more is given."*

You have been given a new mind, a new heart, and eternal life. Now that you have all of that, it is time to share that Good News with someone who desperately needs what you have. Just as Jesus gave himself for your sins, it is time for you to give of yourself that others may know and experience the forgiving love of God.

Read: Acts 1:8

4. Be discipled.

Asking Jesus to become your Savior is the first step to a new life in Christ. Learning to read your Bible is a very important step in growing as a Christian. But in order to really become useful in the kingdom of God, you must become a disciplined learner. The Bible calls this person a disciple of Christ.

When I became a Christian, I asked a friend who was more mature in his Christian faith to disciple me. I asked him to teach me how to live as a Christian and how to read and study the Bible. We memorized Scripture together, witnessed to others, and prayed together. We met every week for two to three hours at a time. This was the most important thing I ever did because it established a strong foundation for my faith.

Read: Matthew 28:19–20

5. Discover your gifts.

When Jesus became your Savior, He filled you with the Holy Spirit. One of the things that He gave you in the process was one or more spiritual gifts. Just as some people have a physical ability to play a sport, sing, or draw pictures better than others, God gives different spiritual talents and abilities to His followers. These spiritual gifts are just waiting for you to use them, but if you don't know which spiritual gifts you have, you will never learn to use them to the best of God's ability. Ask your youth pastor to give you a spiritual gifts test. This will help you understand what your spiritual talents and abilities are, as well as help you better understand how God wants to use you.

Read: 1 Corinthians 12:4–11; 13:1–13

6. Start a Bible club on campus.

When you go to school, look at all of your friends and ask yourself, *"Do they need Jesus?"* Then begin to put into action

123

a plan to get them the message of God's salvation. One option is a Christian or Bible club. Just about every campus has one. Find out where and when the club meets and get involved, but remember, it is vitally important that you not go just to be part of a Christian "holy huddle." You must pray as a group of people who have a passion to reach the rest of the students with the Gospel.

If no club exists, don't be afraid to start one. For information on starting a Bible club, contact my office at Miles Ahead Ministries and ask for the booklet called *My Campus, My Mission*.

Read: Mark 16:15

7. Listen to Christian music.

One of the most effective ways Satan can brainwash you is by pumping trashy music into your head. The words in songs can have a very negative effect on the way you think and act, your moods, and your attitudes. It does not do any good to be singing about killing yourself, having sex, or shooting someone in the back. There is a great deal of good Christian music available for you to listen to. Singing about God—His love and forgiveness and mercy—will truly help God in His attempt to renew your mind.

Read: Psalm 101:1; 150

8. Get a solid Christian friend.

We all have a friend with whom we like to hang out with, but now that you've decided to live your life for Jesus Christ, it is important to find one friend who can become your spiritual partner. The Bible says in Proverbs 18:24, *"There are 'friends' who destroy each other, but a real friend sticks closer than a brother."* God doesn't want you to immediately ditch all your current friends, but He does want you to keep company with someone who can be a spiritual soulmate for you. This is a friend that can pray with you, for you, and someone who you can get discipled by or with.

Read: Ecclesiastes 4:9–12

9. Tithe.

It is very important for you to understand that everything you have was given to you from God—your family, your home, your clothes, and your money. He has also given you the ability to make money by getting a job, or He might have blessed you with a family that gives you an allowance. However you wind up with money, you must realize that it all comes from God. James 1:17 says, *"Whatever is good and perfect comes to us from God above. . . ."*

One of the most important sacrifices you can make is to give ten percent of your money to your church. This not only shows that you are trusting God to provide for your needs, but you are giving back to God what rightfully belongs to Him to be put to use for His glory.

Read: Malachi 3:8–10

10. Start memorizing Scripture.

The Bible says that without faith it is impossible to please God (Hebrews 11:6). The Bible also says that faith comes from hearing the word of God (Romans 10:17).

The more Scripture you know and place your trust in, the stronger your faith will become. Begin memorizing one Scripture verse or passage per week. As your knowledge of the Bible grows, begin memorizing key verses that will help you with a sin you might be struggling with, a problem that keeps coming back to haunt you, or comfort for rough times. Keep a journal of all the verses you memorize and constantly review them.

Read: Psalm 119:9–11

Please complete and return this card to our office to let us know you finished the 21 Jump-Start Program. Have your pastor or spiritual overseer sign the card and return it to Miles Ahead Ministries, 9888 Carroll Center Road #120, San Diego, CA 92126.

Name_____

Address_____

City_____State_____Zip Code_____

Age_____ ❑ Male ❑ Female Telephone (___)_____

Church Attending_____

School Attending_____

I am encouraged to say that_____(your name) has completed the 21 Jump-Start Program.

Pastor's Signature_____

Miles Ahead Crusade Counselor's Information Card

Check One: ❑ Received Christ   ❑ Rededication

Name_____

Address_____

City_____State_____Zip Code_____

Age_____❑ Male ❑ Female Telephone (___)_____

School Attending_____

Do you attend a church? ❑ Yes ❑ No

If yes, church name_____

Did a friend bring you? ❑ Yes ❑ No

If yes, what church does he or she attend?_____